LORCA

MODERN LANGUAGE STUDIES

LORCA

And the Spanish Poetic Tradition

By J. B. TREND

BASIL BLACKWELL
OXFORD
1956

Printed in Great Britain for Basil Blackwell & Mott, Limited
by A. R. Mowbray & Co. Limited in the City of Oxford
and bound at the Kemp Hall Bindery

FOR NATALIA II

POR NATASA II

CONTENTS

LORCA

I

GARCÍA LORCA

I

SOME writers on Lorca can recommend themselves to their readers by the claim that they never met the poet or knew him personally. They mean, I think, that they have not been dazzled by his personality or by a tourist's vision of Granada, and so can see Lorca steadily and see him whole. I have neither of those advantages. I knew Lorca personally when he was beginning, and have been about Spain enough to know that it can never be seen wholly or steadily; while the truth about Granada was apprehended by Lorca himself when he said that it was a 'Paradise closed to many, with gardens open to few': *Paraíso cerrado para muchos, jardines abiertos para pocos*.[1] By accident, or sheer good luck, I happened to be one of those few.

I have described that first meeting with Federico García Lorca before. It sounds, now, too romantic to be true; but it was true in 1919. Granada at that time was living its own life, without tourists; and conditions which seemed to be normal proved afterwards to have been highly exceptional. There was no radio, the gramophone was still a primitive affair with a tin trumpet, and poetry was read aloud or recited among friends. Gardens were open for the performance of poetry and music.

That evening there had been a concert at the Arts Club, the Círculo de Bellas Artes. The performers were a trio of what Shakespeare called 'twangling instruments'; two Spanish lutes and a guitar. Falla, the composer, was there in the audience. Actually it was he who had brought me; and afterwards it seemed that 'of course' we were to go to someone's garden in the oldest and most picturesque part of Granada, the Albaicín. It was already midnight, but we dawdled in the main street, eating prickly pears which someone had bought off a barrow; and then were led up the steep, cobbled streets to a plain door in a high wall. It opened into a large dark garden full of the sound of running water. The three musicians were there and played some of their programme over again, particularly the pieces by Falla. Then a poet was called upon. He declaimed something by Villaespesa; the verse was an unending succession of amphibrachs. Once or twice the reciter hesitated, but he recovered, until the awful moment when he dried up altogether; and a hoarse voice—that type of southern Spanish voice which has grown voiceless from uncounted *cañas* of dry sherry—was heard imitating the rhythm:

¡ Se pierde . . .   se pierde . . .   se pierde . . .   perdió !
¡ *You'll lose it* . . .   *you'll lose it* . . .   *you'll lose it* . . .   *it's lost* !

The audience dissolved in laughter and the poor poet vanished, though he was to be seen afterwards by a trestle table where there were several demijohns—*damajuanas* the Spanish call them—of dry sherry; and a pleasant individual, I remember, embraced me and asked (in German) if I could tell him the publisher of the *Gesammelten Werke* of Walter Pater.

Then we were hushed and a rather shy youth recited. He did not declaim, but spoke in a soft, warm, eager voice: *la obscura, cálida, turbia, inolvidable voz de Federico García Lorca*, Gerardo Diego said long afterwards. It was a simple ballad with striking but easily intelligible imagery. 'Who is it?' 'Federico García Lorca. You must meet him'. The evening ended after 4 a.m., with the poet and myself, arm in arm, helping one another down the steep streets of the Albaicín, to the main street and the bottom of the Alhambra Hill. ¡ *Noche, que noche nochera* !

That was my introduction to modern Spanish poetry. It was followed a year later by a book called *Libro de poemas*, with an autograph inscription—a precious book which is kept out of sight at the back of a bookshelf. Soon after that I reviewed the book, in an article which an American bibliographer has claimed to be the first ever published outside Spain on Federico García Lorca. Later the review was re-written for a book, and I should like to quote from it now.

A stray traveller (it said) should be the last to claim that he has discovered a new poet. I must confess, indeed, that I opened Sr. García Lorca's book with certain misgivings. I had made the acquaintance of his poetry . . . in circumstances which were so exceptional . . . that they seemed never likely to be repeated. I was afraid of meeting it again in cold print. In that corner of Europe to which the poet belongs, poetry, like music, is a thing to be performed. It is read aloud in gardens on summer nights. . . . in surroundings which are like Mr. Walter de la Mare's 'Arabia' come true. To understand García Lorca, an English reader must begin by saying that exquisite English poem over to himself. He must 'decry her gliding streams', he must

> Hear her strange lutes on the green banks
> Ring loud with the grief and delight
> Of the dim-silked, dark-haired Musicians
> In the brooding silence of night.

That was the background against which García Lorca's poetry was performed. The experience of it, therefore, was a composite experience; the printed page of to-day is only a part.

This, of course, is begging the question. A poet has no right to expect you to know his own particular corner of the world. But he has the right to expect you to look at things from his point of view—if you can; and to assume that you know something of what his contemporaries are doing: especially his older contemporaries. You must try to realize his poetic environment, and discover what sort of poetry he was likely to have heard and read.

The poetic environment of a Spanish poet at that time might be said to consist of two gliding streams. There were the nursery rhymes, the singing games, and the short, epigrammatic *cantares*: and those, in García Lorca's home in 'Arabia', people sang to a guitar—not the guitar of national legend, but a guitar played seriously as a serious instrument. On the other side were Rubén Darío and Villaespesa, with contemporary poets like Antonio Machado and his brother Manuel, Enrique de Mesa, Valle-Inclán and Juan Ramón Jiménez. The field was wide—wide as Spain and Spanish-speaking America; and there was plenty of room for poets to cultivate their own corners of it independently. García Lorca's corner was a place of trees and falling water, of dreams, and children playing.

Poetry was a social, friendly accomplishment, natural to the society into which García Lorca was born; and later, in Montevideo, he told another poet that he wrote poetry because he wanted people to like him; and that, too, was part of the explanation of his poetry.[2]

It is difficult for a foreigner to judge (the review went on) but these verses seem less reminiscent than many first books of verse. There are reminiscences, of course; but they are reminiscences of sound rather than of sense. . . . It is seldom that this poet writes the poetry of other people's poetry, or the erotic mysticism of other people's passions; and he never uses forms that have to be filled out with padding. There is a curious distinction about his writing; yet it is combined, as a rule, with an engaging simplicity.

That review was a youthful indiscretion: a shot in the dark, perhaps—or in a dark garden at Granada—but I do not wish to withdraw it. I did not know at the time—indeed, it has hardly yet been realized outside the Spanish-speaking countries—that García Lorca was not alone. He was, in fact, or became later, a member of, a brilliant circle of contemporary Spanish poets, the most brilliant for three hundred years; though now, in consequence of the Civil War and the persecution which followed it, nearly all those poets are either dead or in exile, while one of the best books about them is called *Tríptico del Sacrificio* (a triptych of the sacrifice) by Guillermo de Torre who afterwards edited the complete works of García Lorca in Buenos Aires.

This revival of Spanish poetry followed the revival of the novel which began in 1868; the best pages and most typical characters of Pérez Galdós, though still (with two recent exceptions) largely untranslated, are to my mind almost on a level with the great Russians. After the novel came the essay. The condition of staleness and frustration which led to defeat in the Spanish-American war of 1898 stimulated Unamuno and contemporary essayists to some of their best writing; while the new sympathy of the Spanish-speaking American countries for the people of Spain disposed Spaniards to read the Central American poet Rubén Darío. Darío had revolutionized Spanish prosody, something in the way that Swinburne had revolutionized prosody in English; and though poets in Spain did not follow him in his Parisian Greek subjects or his expansive Spanish-American manner, they learnt from him how to write alexandrines and hexameters and other forms of verse which had been little used in Spanish. On the formal side, they nearly all began to write like Rubén Darío, though on the other side they were more like their own poet, essayist and philosophical writer, Unamuno; and Unamuno, though he wrote sonnets as if he were heaving bricks at a wall, yet had his roots firmly planted in the soil of Spain and in his own everyday Spanish thoughts.

The first result of the new poetry in Spain was Juan Ramón Jiménez. Though some of his early alexandrines sound like Rubén Darío, he soon became something very different; more finished, more subtle and more penetrating, with a poetical world of his own; and he is still the central figure among contemporary Spanish poets, though frowned on in Madrid for preferring exile to the régime of General Franco. Then were was Antonio Machado, who developed in directions where he met no one else. He followed the winding galleries of his own mind, the wide and windy uplands of Castille, the social satire on certain types in Andalucía, and the premature existentialist philosophy of a great teacher who was entirely imaginary, and invented by the poet himself.

Lorca belonged to a younger generation. He was born near Granada at the end of the nineteenth century—he liked to keep the date unspecified—and there is little or nothing of Rubén Darío about him, even on the rare occasions (such as the Ode to Salvador Dalí) when he wrote alexandrines. Like his contemporaries, his favourite verse was the characteristic eight-syllable line with varying accentuation—'hovering stresses', Mr. MacNeice calls them—and assonance: rhyming on the vowels but not on the consonants. That use of assonance instead of full rhyme has been one of the great advantages which poetry in Spanish has had over the poetry of almost all modern languages. In English, we are only just beginning to use it, and still finding that imperfect rhymes or 'pararhymes' in the style of Wilfred Owen may suit us better; but in Spain, assonance has been used by poets for eight hundred years. Assonance does not exclude rhyme, which is valued for certain effects; but it saves poetry from the abuse of rhyme in a language where rhyming is too easy and almost always feminine and two-syllabled, while it helps to keep verse natural and within speaking distance of people in general.

What distinguished Lorca from his contemporaries was that he followed every suggestion and evocation which word or verse could give him. That led him to popular verse and also to plays in verse, but above all it led him to ballads; and his book of ballads about gipsy ways and the 'gipsified' customs of Southern Spain, the *Romancero gitano*, will probably be his most enduring achievement.

2

Most readers and critics of García Lorca have tried to place him in the Spain of the 'black legend': the Spain of blood, lust, death and all the 'isms'. I confess that, from my first long visit to Spain in 1919 down to the Civil War of 1936, I took things in Spain as I found them. I regarded Spanish things and Spanish ways as natural, and did not go about looking for 'isms'. In 1919, after four and a half years in uniform, Spanish ways seemed not only natural but friendly and delightful; for even the 1914–18 war was a crescendo of horrors, and the fearful casualties among one's friends made Spain seem not a country of war and lechery, but of a new Age of Reason.

The new Age of Reason has not yet arrived. At this moment it seems further off than ever; and what we have now is an age of mysticism, showing itself incidentally in unscientific psycho-analysis and unconvincing popular theology. There is room for both of these if they are real and genuine; but neither of them can help us to tell a good poem from a bad one, and attempts to make deductions from Lorca's poems by amateur psycho-analysis or popular theology are apt to mislead, if not checked by evidence from other sources. The word *verde* (green), for instance, has been taken for a psycho-analytical symbol. Actually, when Lorca said that a thing was green, we knew that it *was* green, and that was that; it did not occur to us that he was consciously or deliberately symbolizing anything. The ballads on Tamar and Santa Olalla, again have been brought forward in evidence of Lorca's preoccupation with sex; and above all there is the ballad of the faithless wife: *La casada infiel*.[3] In fact, the point of that poem is the high gipsy standard of manners. The gipsy, looking back on the affair in a cool hour, considers that he acted correctly, *como gitano legítimo*. He made his companion a present afterwards. 'But I didn't know she was married.' The Lorca I knew was certainly not over-sexed. On the contrary.

The story of Tamar—'Atamares' of the gipsies—came originally from the Old Testament; she was the sister of Absalom, but was forced by her half-brother Amnon. An earlier Tamar was married to Onan, and afterwards solicited her father-in-law, Judah. The first of these edifying stories was sung to children of the well-to-do by their nurses who came from remote villages. The poet tells us so himself. There is a ballad about it, which was sung to put children to sleep. The grim and bloodthirsty words of Spanish cradle-songs have been remarked; but are they any more blood-thirsty than our own?—that well-loved rhyme for instance, for playing 'Oranges and Lemons':

> Here comes a candle to light you to bed,
> And here comes a chopper to chop off your head.

Lorca's gipsy ballads did not come first. The *Libro de poemas* of 1921 prepares the scene. The *Canciones* (1921–24, published in 1927) gradually introduce human figures; and human figures are there, in all their full-blooded life, in the *Romancero gitano* (begun in 1924,

but not published until 1928) and in the *Poema del cante jondo* of 1931.
These poems fill the scene, already prepared in the earlier volumes,
with real people; gipsies, horse-copers, smugglers, civil guards; and
the civil guards are only too real, even though their souls—like
their three-cornered hats—are (Lorca said) made of patent leather:
almas de charol. Yet the ballads are all—and one is actually called
that—*romances sonámbulos*⁴: sleep-walking ballads. Life is still a
dream. The gipsies are formed from bronze and sleep, *bronce y
sueño.*

Lorca came from a family of large and successful farmers. His
mother had been a school-teacher; but among his aunts and uncles
were people extremely well-acquainted with popular poetry. He
spent eleven years—nearly a third of his life—in university colleges.
The first was the Residencia de Estudiantes at Madrid (1918–28)
where he met the most prominent poets of his generation; for the
President of that College, Don Alberto Jiménez, besides being an
ideal head of a house, had the genius to attract to it many of the
best poets of the time. It was the poet Juan Ramón Jiménez who
had designed the gardens between the College buildings; and
Unamuno was often to be seen and heard there, during his visits
to Madrid, particularly after his return from exile in 1931. Antonio
Machado and Alfonso Reyes were frequent visitors; so were Enrique
de Mesa and Pérez de Ayala; while Moreno Villa, Pedro Salinas,
Jorge Guillén, Emilio Prados were all at one time or another actually
in residence at the College, together with Buñuel and a painter who
had considerable influence on Lorca: Salvador Dalí.

Then, after ten years' desultory study of what were known in
Spain as 'Philosophy and Letters', Lorca moved to America. It is
said that he went there because he had made a mess of his love-
affairs. That may be or may not; the same has been said of Rupert
Brooke. Lorca spent a year at Columbia University, New York.
To him, the American scene and the American way of life were
shattering—far more than they had been to Rupert Brooke, or
to Juan Ramón Jiménez in 1915. It was all so 'un-Latin'. The only
kindred spirit among the poets was the ghost of Walt Whitman,
with his beard full of butterflies, Lorca said:

tu barba, llena de mariposas.

The only part of New York he really liked was the negro part,
Harlem. His book, *Poeta en Nueva York*, profoundly influenced by
Whitman in form and deeply tinged by surrealism in approach,

is taken by many foreign critics for his most important poetic
achievement. It may be; but I am inclined to agree with Guillermo
de Torre that *Poeta en Nueva York* is really a work of transition.
He was certainly doing what other poets of the time were doing,
in Europe and America; but these poems are the saddest and most
tragic he ever wrote. The poet in New York was a lost soul.
Confirmation for this view can be found in another Spanish critic,
José Bergamín, who edited the first edition of *Poeta en Nueva York*,
in Mexico in 1940. He regards it as 'a borderland book', *un libro
fronterizo*:

> The words (he says) have not the same clear and exact value that they have
> in the best poems. . . . While he sings, he stammers words of terror, which
> suddenly seem to become cradle-songs; but the thing he rocks in his arms is
> some inhuman creature: a dead dog or a dead chicken. . . . The poet in New York
> once the poet in Granada, remembering his lost Paradise of streams and skies . . .
> but now alone in a strange city, becomes a child once more; he would scream,
> if he could, in his immense, lethal nightmare.

Lorca fled from New York, and reached Havana, waltzing, he
said, towards civilization. In Cuba he found himself at home once
more; not only because Cuba speaks Spanish, but because the
coloured people there are so much happier and more natural than
they are in the north. 'We Latins', the Mulatto Cuban poet,
Nicolás Guillén, said to him. He breathed again.

It is usual, in speaking of García Lorca, to point out how he turned
away from 'culture' and sought the society of singers and dancers.
He certainly had a passion for *cante jondo* or *cante andaluz*—the 'deep
song' of southern Spain—and wrote a book of poems inspired by it.
But a passion for *cante jondo* is not turning away from culture.
Many 'cultured' people have frequented the performance, and—
if they were able—the society, of Andalusian singers and dancers,
not because they were tired of 'culture', but because they wished
to acquire something of the oldest culture in the Peninsula. There
is no room for conjecture about this; Lorca has told us quite clearly
what went to the formation of his poetry and his mind, and popular
poetry had a large share in it. It did not begin with *cante jondo*,
however, but with the kind of poetry known in Victorian England
as 'nursery rhymes'. *Nanas*, he called them, *nanas infantiles*: songs
sung by a mother to put her baby to sleep. In the late 'twenties,
Lorca went about Spain collecting *nanas*, and formed the impression
that, in Spain, they 'use melodies of the most melancholy and blood-
thirsty description'. That we have seen, applies to other countries

too. The chief singers of these songs, he found, were the women who went out for nurses.

These nurses and domestic servants have long been performing the important task of bringing ballads, songs and stories to the houses of the well-to-do. The old ballads of Gerineldo, Don Bernardo del Carpio, Tamar, the Lovers of Teruel—children hear all these from those admirable nurses and maids who come down from the mountains or up from the rivers to give us our first lessons in Spanish history.[5]

García Lorca described this to an audience at Havana with such simplicity and conviction that it must have been what happened in his own home at Fuente Vaqueros, in the country near Granada.

The mother or nurse often turns the song into an abstract landscape, almost always at night, and there she puts—like the oldest and simplest interludes and mystery plays—one or two characters who perform some simple dramatic action, generally with the finest but most melancholy effect that can possibly be imagined.[6]

On this diminutive stage come the types which will stay in the child's head for the rest of its life: the man who led his horse down to the water, but left him with nothing to drink

> de aquél
> que llevó el caballo al agua
> y le dejó sin beber.

Or the man who tried to feed his horse 'on the leaves of a green lemon, and he wouldn't eat them at all'.

> A mi caballo le eché
> hojitas de limón verde,
> y no las quiso comer.

The mother (Lorca said) evokes a landscape by the most simple means, and makes a personage pass across it whom she hardly ever names; . . . and the child has a poetic game of pure beauty before going to sleep. 'That man' and his horse go off into the distance along the road under the dark branches down to the river, and he comes back to ride again whenever the song begins once more. The child never sees him face to face. It always imagines him in the shadow: the man's dark clothes and the bright-coloured saddle-blanket.

No one in these songs ever shows his face. They must go off into the distance and take the road to places where the water is deeper, and the birds will never fly any more.

In other songs the child recognizes the man, knows him by sight; for the outline of his figure is familiar—even his features and the flat curl on the forehead, like Antonio Torres Heredia in one

B

of the gipsy ballads. But it is a world of poetry inaccessible to us: one without a grain of reason to destroy it

... where (Lorca says, in a way very characteristic of him) the white horse, half nickel and half smoke, suddenly falls wounded with a swarm of bees buzzing furiously over his eyes.

Sometimes mother and child themselves go off on an adventure.

Danger threatens. We have to grow smaller and smaller; the walls of the hut touch us all the way round. Outside they're watching us. We have to live in a very small space. If we could, we should live in an orange, you and I. Or better in a grape. . . . And at that point sleep comes.

It is fascinating to find Federico García Lorca describing the formation of his own poetry from the ways he has heard mothers and nurses put their babies to sleep. It applies to his earlier poems; it applies to his ballads, and seems like a description of what the mother is saying to her baby in the first act of his play, *Bodas de sangre*. One of the ballads is called *Romance sonámbulo*, 'a sleep-walking ballad'. But all of them are that: all have dream-vision and dream-logic, and the dream is induced by the poet telling the story to put us into a condition in which dream-vision and dream-logic are only natural. That applies to nearly all Lorca's poems, not only the ballads, but the ballads are the best examples.

ROMANCE DE LA LUNA, LUNA

The moon came down to the smithy, crinoline of tuberoses. The child was looking and looking, the child kept on looking. The air grew more and more excited; the moon kept moving her arms, and showed, lascivious yet pure, her hard and tinny bosom.

'Moon, moon, run away! If the gipsies found you here, they would steal your heart to make their metal rings and collars.'

'Child, let me dance awhile! If the gipsies really come, they would find you on the anvil with both of your eyes shut tight.'

'Moon, moon, run away! Now I hear their horses coming.'

'Go away, don't put your feet on my stiff and starchy whiteness.'

Nearer, nearer, came the horsemen, drumming the drum of the plain. In the smithy, the small boy was waiting with eyes shut tight. Through the olive-grove they came, bronze and dream: they were gipsies. Their heads were thrown back proudly, but their eyes were all turned inwards. How the little owl was hooting there, as it sat on a bough! Through the sky the moon was marching, while a small boy held her hand.

But there were tears in the smithy, tears and shouting: they were gipsies. And the air was watching, watching; the air kept watching her go.

Romancero gitano

The *Romance sonámbulo* plays on the Spanish overtones of the word for 'green', like an early poem of Juan Ramón Jiménez. Yet the feeling is essentially Lorca, with a suggestion of Falla's ballet *El amor brujo*.

ROMANCE SONÁMBULO

Green, green, how I love you! Green wind, green branches. The ship far out on the sea, and the horse upon the mountains.

With the shadow in her girdle, dreaming at her window-bar, green cheeks and green hair, and eyes of the cold silver.

Green, green, how I love you!

Under the gipsy moon, things turn to look in her eyes, yet she cannot see them too.

Green, green, how I love you!

See the great stars of hoar-frost, coming with pitch-dark shadows, opening the road to dawn. Now the fig-tree strokes the wind with the smoothness of its branches; the mountain's a thieving wild-cat, fur on end with cactus prickles.

But who's that? How could he get there?

Still she's at her window-bar, green cheeks and green hair, dreaming in seas of bitterness.

'Neighbour, I would change with you: change a good horse for your house, change my saddle for your mirror, my long knife for your blanket. Neighbour, bleeding all the way, I come from the passes of Cabra.'

'If only I could, young man; here's a deal that's quickly done. But I am no longer I, and my house is not my house.'

'Neighbour, neighbour, let me die, decently and in a bed. An iron bedstead let it be, and the sheets be linen sheets. See the gaping wound I have from my navel to my neck.'

'Ay, three hundred roses red, frill the front of your shirt; and I smell the smell of blood, oozing round about your sash. But I am no longer I, and my house is not my house.'

'Let me go up, at least, to the high barred window: Let me go up, let me pass to the high green window; to the window-bars of the moon and the roaring waterfalls.'

Then the two neighbours went up to the high barred window, leaving a trail of blood, leaving a trail of tears; while the little tin lanterns trembled there on the roof, and a thousand drums of crystal beat on the early morning.

Green, green, how I love you! Green wind, green branches.

So the two neighbours went up, and the wide wind left with them a rare taste in the mouth, of gall and mint and sweet basil.

'Neighbour, neighbour, tell me now, where is your daughter, bitter-sweet? How long shall I wait for you! How long, how long have I waited! That pale face, that coal-black hair, at the green window bar!'

Out on the edge of the cistern the gipsy girl was swinging. Green cheeks and green hair, and eyes of the cold silver. An icicle from the moon held her above the water.

The night had become friendly like the turn of a back street. The Civil Guards
were drunk when they came and knocked at the door.
    Green, green, how I love you! Green wind, green branches! The ship far
out on the sea, and the horse upon the mountains.

Romancero gitano[7]

Yet this is a ballad. The gipsies are not only bronze and dream;
they have knives. There has been a fight, a *reyerta*; and the girl's
lover is bleeding to death. 'Señores', the Civil Guards are told in
another ballad, 'here it has been the old, old story. The dead were
four of them Romans, with five that were Carthaginians.'

> Señores guardias civiles:
> aquí pasó lo de siempre.
> Han muerto cuatro romanos
> y cinco cartagineses.

The ballad of the martyrdom of Santa Olalla (Eulalia) begins
with a reference to a roughly illustrated religious leaflet—a 'tract',
almost—showing Flora, stark naked, ascending 'a little old stairway
of water':

> Flora desnuda se sube
> por escalerillas de aqua

The diminutive *-illas* does not mean that the stairs are particularly
narrow, but that the poet had an affectionate feeling for them: a
memory, perhaps, of those in the garden of Generalife, where the
water runs down the banisters. The same love of diminutives can
be heard in the everyday speech of Argentina, Chile, and Mexico:
adiosito, 'goodbye, my dear'; *ahorita*, 'I'll do it for you in a moment';
despacito, 'gently, gently'. The Romans knew this way of speaking,
too, and called it CAPTATIO BENEVOLENTIAE; to Lorca it came
naturally. We never find him 'talking bronco'.

3

Lorca, from the first, was fascinated by what children sing in the
streets. Granada is—or used to be—full of the sounds of falling
water and children playing; and it was a blend of those two sounds
that reached you if you leant over the walls of the Alhambra. 'Clear
runs the river, oh!—fountains are falling.'

> Arroyo claro,
> Fuente serena[8]

You feel that Lorca would have given everything to have been the only begetter of a real Spanish 'nursery' rhyme like that, or a piece of pure verbal magic like 'Moon, moon—bells in the moon'

> Luna, lunera
> cascabelera.

Even the grim Unamuno fell to this, though on his rough tongue it turned to bitterness: 'Moon, moon—lunatic moon'

> luna, lunera, lunática.

The poetry of children's games was frequently an inspiration to Lorca like the poetry of cradle-songs. The 'Ballad of a day in July' is unintelligible, unless one knows the game of *Viudita*, the Widow. In that game, a ring of children dance round the 'widow', who sings:

> Yo soy la viudita   Oh, I am a widow,
> del conde Laurel,   The Countess Laurelle,
> que quiero casarme: I want to be married;
> no encuentro con quién.   To whom, I can't tell.

The ring of children answers; and the widowed countess, looking round the circle of intense Spanish faces says: 'I choose . . . you!' making a dive for the chosen one who becomes the countess in her turn.

García Lorca brought this into his early ballad of a July day— it was in 1919—when, to the tinkle of silver cow-bells, a voice asks:

> 'Where are you going to, my pretty maid,
>   All sun and snow?'
>
> 'I'm going to pick daisies, sir,' she said,
>   'In the green meadow.'
>
> 'The meadow is very fearful
>   And far from here.'
>
> 'For the rough wind and deep shade
>   My love has no fear.'
>
> 'He'll fear the sun, my pretty maid,
>   All sun and snow.'
>
> 'But he has gone from my sight
>   Now long ago.'
>
> 'Who are you, then, fair maid,
>   And where is your home?'

'From deep loves and fountains
    Do I come.'

(A tinkle of silver cow-bells)

'What have you got on your lips
    That burn so red?'

'The star of my true-love,
    Who's alive, yet dead.'

'What do you bear in your bosom,
    So light and fine?'

'The sword of my true-love,
    Who's dead, yet alive.'

'What have you got in your eyes,
    As black as jet?'

'The sorrow of my thoughts
    That wound me yet.'

'Why do you wear that mantle,
    As black as death?'

'Oh, I'm a widow, gentle sir,
    In want and sorrow.
My true-love, he was Count Laurelle
    Lord of the Laurel.'

'But who are you looking for, my pretty maid,
    If you've no lover?'

'I seek the body of Count Laurelle,
    Lord of the Laurel.'

'So then, you look for a lover,
    My pretty widow?
You look for a lover too far,
    For I am with you.'

'The stars of heaven are my delight,
    Oh, sir,' she said.
'But where can I find my own true-love,
    Alive or dead?'

'Your true-love, he lies in the stream, pretty maid,
    All sun and snow;
With maiden pinks about his head,
    And his great sorrow.'

'Alas, my wandering knight-at-arms
  Of the cypress tree,
One night beneath the moon, your soul
  You offered me.'

'Oh, Isis of my long dream,
  Maid without honey;
You, in the speech of children,
  Your dream have told me.
My heart I offer you,
  A heart that's human;
One wounded by the eyes
  Of every woman.'

'Oh, knight of gallantry,
  Good-bye to you.
I go to look for Count Laurelle,
  My love so true.'

'Good-bye, good-bye, my pretty maid,
  Rose ever sleeping,
You go to look for your true-love,
  And I for dying.

        (*A tinkle of silver cow-bells*)

My heart will bleed to death
Like the stream below.'

                              Libro de poemas[9]

That sort of poetry is not Federico Lorca's great poetry—not
his final achievement—but it was the everyday stuff out of which
much of his mature poetry grew. Yet it is misleading. The version
given above is not translation, but transplantation; it is Lorca
transplanted from Granada to England: a Spanish tune harmonized
like an English folksong, and translators ought *not* to do that sort
of thing. They should resist the temptation of turning these poems
into an English which gives all the wrong associations. Lorca's
poems, if ever they are to be translated adequately, must be put
into an English which (the phrase comes from R. C. Trevelyan) is
'disinfected' from all English suggestions; only then can it convey
the exotic suggestion of the original Spanish. One must firmly
avoid both English rhyme and Scottish ballad-metre.[10] To my mind
the most successful translations, so far, are those of Stephen Spender
and J. L. Gili; yet this literal version, with some attempt at conveying

the vowel-harmony of the original, and beautifully printed with the Spanish on the opposite page, seems—to Spanish readers— 'colourless'. They miss the rhythm. Actually, the rhythm is the one thing which an English translator can follow, and more or less reproduce. Translation of Lorca's poems should, above all, be rhythmical, following as far as possible the movement of the original. The ideal English version would be one which would fit a setting of the original Spanish to music.

Lorca's poems were recited—first to friends, and then in public— long before they were printed. His poetry is for the ear, not for the eye; and that should be taken into consideration by those who translate him. But one thing in his poetry is frankly untranslatable: the verbal magic. In this respect the recent Spanish poets have all been conscious of their forerunners; particularly the Renaissance poets Garcilaso and Góngora, and the primitive poets of the Middle Ages. Some of the early Spanish poems—some of the refrains of the early Spanish poems—are little more than jingles: delightful jingles signifying nothing. That is true of a great deal of primitive and popular poetry; but there is a magic, too, in the mere sound of Spanish words, however charged with meaning and association they may be now. Mallarmé wrote to Degas that sonnets were not made with ideas, but with words; and in medieval Spain (and in later times too) words themselves have an effect, a power, a magic, which no amount of 'meaning' can explain away. The sound may mean more than the sense. The poetry is not in the meaning, but in the evocation.

There remains the imagery; and that, a translation should be able to convey. Lorca's imagery came originally from popular poetry and children's games; and also from the semi-popular poetry of an earlier age, which, in his time, was being recovered from the sixteenth-century music-books. It often has the *curiosa felicitas* of country speech. Then Lorca found that Góngora had done the same thing. He saw that language is formed on a basis of imagery, and that the people in his part of the world—Granada and the south of Spain generally—had a magnificent wealth of imagery. 'Green voices', for instance. We should say now that they were an invention of García Lorca; but they are already in Góngora. So are the hours all 'dressed-up in numbers', *las horas ya de números vestidos*; and eyes like Federico's own 'with much night in them': *los ojos con mucha noche*. Yet those are in Góngora too; while the phrase 'an ox of a river', *un buey de agua*, an Andalucian image admired by Lorca and extolled by all his critics for its startling originality, had already been used by Horace and before him by Sophocles.[11] It is old, and Mediterranean; for rivers flowing down from the mountains in Mediterranean countries rush like a bull, in spring, though in summer they run bone-dry or a little trickle in the sand.

Lorca was a man whose strongest impressions were visual. In this, he was like other Spanish poets of his time, like Rafael Alberti, whose first thought was to be a cubist painter; like Juan Ramón Jiménez, who worked in a studio at Seville, and like Moreno Villa of whom it would be hard to say whether he was primarily a painter or a poet. García Lorca's metaphors are almost always conditioned by sight. So are the metaphors of cradle-songs. It is a view which limits the field of vision and gives it a sharper outline, though it foreshortens the perspective and concentrates the light, like a view through prismatic glasses. One thinks of Keats, doing much the same thing. Lorca knew that too. His knowledge of English was limited, yet he divined that Keats had concentrated his vision in the same way. He wrote—rather oddly—that

. . . even the most evanescent (*sic*) English poets, like Keats, must draw an outline and limit their metaphors and figurations; and Keats is saved, by his admirable plastic sense, from the dangerous poetical world of his visions.

'Imagery', he said later, in a talk on Góngora at the Residencia de Estudiantes, 'is a change of dress or occupation, between things and ideas.'

They have their own planes and their own orbits; but metaphor joins them through the imagination taking a high fence on horse-back (*un salto equestre de la imaginación*) . . . The poet harmonizes two different worlds, and gives them plastic form, in a way that may often seem violent; but in his hands there is no disorder nor disproportion. He holds, like toys, seas and geographical kingdoms and hurricane winds.[12]

Francis Thompson said much the same of Shelley in his famous essay in the passage beginning: 'The universe is his box of toys'. Lorca's religious imagery, also, is that of a child. Rather than from the statues in country churches, it came from the domestic plaster saints on the family altar or chest of drawers, and the little clay figures which children put into their toy 'Bethlehems' (*nacimientos*) at Christmas. There were also the rough woodcuts on those broadsheets which used to appear at certain seasosn of the year, and were known as *aleluyas*.

4

To the end, Lorca kept something of the wide-eyed wonder of a
child, in a world where many of the others were mad.

> I said: 'Why, it's afternoon!'
> But it wasn't.
> The afternoon was something else
> which had already gone.
>   (And the daylight
> shrugged its shoulders like a girl.)
>
> It's afternoon! But no, it's no use!
> This is a sham one; this has
> a half moon like lead.
> The other won't come back ever.
>   (And the daylight—we all saw it—
> played at being a statue with the mad boy.)
>
> That one was little,
> and munched a pomegranate.
> This one is biggish and green, and I can't
> take her in my arms or dress her.
>   Won't she come back? Why won't she?
>   (And the daylight, as it went—for a joke—
> separated the mad boy from his shadow.)

Canciones[13]

CAMPANA

> In the tower,
> the yellow tower,
> a bell is tolling.
> In the wind,
> the yellow wind,
> bell-notes everywhere falling.
>
> Stroke of resounding dagger,
> opening a wound in the distance.
> And yet they tremble, like
> the breasts of girls playing.
> In the tower,
> the yellow tower,
> now the bell stops ringing.
>
> The air out of the dust,
> is making ships of silver.

Poema del cante jondo[14]

CANCIÓN DEL JINETE

Córdoba.
Far-off and lonely.

Coal-black mare and big full moon;
Olives in my saddle-bag,
Even though I know the roads,
I'll never come to Córdoba.

Along the plain, along the wind,
Coal-black mare and blood-red moon.
Death's always watching me now
From the towers of Córdoba.

Alas for the long long road!
Alas for the valiant mare!
Alas for the death that awaits me
Before I come to Córdoba.

Córdoba.
Far-off and lonely.

Poema del cante jondo[15]

No child was ever more affectionate than Lorca, or could inspire more affection in others. I repeat the remark: 'I write poetry because I want people to like me', that he made to a friend in Montevideo. Yet the writing of poetry was a serious business, the most serious thing in life.

'The poet who is going to write a poem', Lorca said—and added that he knew it from his own experience—'has the vague sensation of going to a nocturnal hunting-party in a wood a long way away. An unaccountable fear whispers in his heart. To calm himself, it is always useful for him to drink a glass of cold water, and make black pen-strokes with no meaning.'

Lorca kept his head, and held on tight, even in the most over-powering moments; and he was always very careful of his technique.

'I am not unconscious of what I am doing', he told Gerardo Diego, the editor of an admirable anthology. 'On the contrary, if it's true that I'm a poet by the grace of God—or the devil—it is also true that I'm one by the grace of technique and effort, and of knowing exactly what a poem is.'[16]

Poetry (he said) felt like fire in his hands; yet he understood it and could work with it perfectly. *Mira. Yo tengo el fuego en mis manos. Yo lo entiendo y trabajo con él perfectamente.*

His most complete account of poetic inspiration came in a lecture

at Havana: Theory and practice of the *duende*, or familiar spirit.[17]
In many parts of Spain there was a saying 'He has a *duende*' or 'has
much *duende*'. 'You have a voice', a young Andalucian singer was
told—a singer of *cante jondo*. 'You know the styles; but you will
never have a success, because you have no *duende*'. In Andalucía
people talked perpetually of the *duende*, for they found it in whatever
came out with the irresistible effectiveness of instinct. An elderly
gipsy dancer exclaimed one day, on hearing a record of the pianist,
Brailowsky, playing Bach: '*Ole*! That has a *duende*'; but she was
unmoved by Gluck, Brahms or Darius Milhaud. And Miguel
Torres, the gipsy, 'the man with the greatest culture in the blood
I have ever known', Lorca said, declared when he heard Falla playing
one of his *Nights in the gardens of Spain*: 'Everything that has black
sounds has the *duende*'. These black sounds, needless to say, have
nothing to do with the black notes on the piano. They are the
mystery, 'the roots (Lorca said) held fast in the primitive slime we
all know (but which none of us really knows) from which comes
everything that is substantial in art'. The *duende* is not quite *das
Dämonische* which Goethe told Eckermann he found in the playing
of Paganini. Nor should anyone confuse it with the demon of
theological doubt at which Luther threw a bottle of ink; or with
the conventional devil of popular theology, which Lorca thought
so absurd and unintelligent because he disguised himself as a little
dog to get into convents.

The duende (he said) is a power, not a method; a struggle, not a thought. . . .
It is not in the gipsy's singer's throat, but rises from within him, from the soles
of his feet. . . . For every artist, every step he climbs in the tower of perfection
costs him a struggle—not with the angel, or with the muse, but with the *duende*.[18]

Falla had the *duende* and Juan Ramón Jiménez has it; but in few
has it risen so often from the soles of the feet to produce the 'black
sounds' that we get in Federico García Lorca.

The *duende* rises unmistakably in many of the plays. If he had
lived, Lorca would have been the poet who returned Spanish poetic
drama to the heights where it was left by Lope de Vega; for after his
lyrics and ballads, Lorca's highest flights were in tragedy; and *Bodas
de sangre*, *Yerma* and *La casa de Bernarda Alba* have restored tragedy
to the Spanish stage. Many of his plays suggest the Irish plays of
Synge, both in the language that people talk and the kind of people
who talk it. (An English writer in the Argentine, Mr. Patrick
Dudgeon, first pointed this out.) Lorca is unlikely to have known

Synge in the original; but there is an excellent Spanish translation of *Riders to the Sea* ('Jinetes hacia el mar') by Juan Ramón Jiménez. It came out about 1920, and Lorca is bound to have read it; there is, in fact, an extraordinary likeness between the mother in *Bodas de sangre* and the mother in *Riders to the Sea*. Their thoughts run on the same lines and they say much the same things. One thing is clear, at any rate: the proper language for translating Lorca's plays is Anglo-Irish. Yet one looks in vain for that beautiful choice of simple words, and those appealing Anglo-Irish cadences, in the translations of Lorca's plays that are printed and performed.

Yerma and *Bodas de Sangre* were great experiences when one saw them on the stage; and so was the interpretation of Margarita Xirgu, who showed from the first that she believed in the poet, and did not, like some others, insist upon alterations. *Yerma*, another of his interpreters said, was the tragedy of Federico himself.[19] Again, the early play, *Mariana Pineda*, is also a beautiful and moving experience. It already shows the poet's power over the ballad; and incidentally gives the lie to those who would like us to believe that he had no political convictions. The play was, in fact, produced at a time when it could only have been taken for a protest against the dictatorship of Primo de Rivera. In a way the whole of Lorca's theatre is a political conviction, or at any rate a social service; and his *Barraca*—a travelling or fit-up theatre—was 'a theatre for everybody', like the Old Vic; a protest and a contrast to the commercial Spanish theatre, where it used to be impossible—and once more seems to be impossible—to perform Lope or Calderón or any of the great plays of the past without copious additions or *refundiciones*. Lorca proved, with his amateur or semi-professional *Barraca*, that Lope de Vega has only to be put straight on the stage, by intelligent people of good will, to have an overwhelming effect on a modern audience. *Fuente Ovejuna* and *Peribáñez*, produced by García Lorca, had a message for a Spanish audience of the 'thirties, which neither their original creator, nor any subsequent producer, is likely to feel again. 'He sat on the grass in a circle of blue dungarees', one of them told me, 'the student members of *La Barraca* theatre workshop, who did *Fuente Ovejuna* in the open air.'

Lorca achieved the height of his poetic expression in his lament for the bull-fighter Sánchez Mejías. This is not merely a piece of local colour or traditional *popularismo*. Sánchez Mejías was no ordinary bull-fighter, though he had reached the top of his profession. He had written an original and successful play; he was a fine and noble character and enjoyed the friendship not only of García Lorca and Rafael Alberti, but of other poets and writers of their generation. So, too, had the cattle-breeder Francisco Villalón who, after writing some shorter poems which derive (though not too closely) from one of the earlier manners of García Lorca, suddenly revealed himself as a most original poet, with *La Toríada* (The Toriad), an epic, in the language of Góngora, on the life of wild bulls in the long grass of their native pastures. Villalón was a poet, even in his professional relations. He declared that he had always had an ambition to breed a bull with green eyes, and he lost a fortune over it.

The death of Sánchez Mejías in the ring brought consternation to his friends; but it led to two of the finest poems in modern Spanish literature: the *Llanto* (Lament) of García Lorca and the *Elegía* of Rafael Alberti. Both poems are in several movements like a symphony; Lorca's four movements in different metres are a summing-up of his whole poetic achievement. The first has one short line repeated like a bell; though it is so plain a statement of fact—the time of day—that he may have read it first in a newspaper. The second is in the traditional Spanish ballad form; the third, in the long lines of Spanish alexandrines; the fourth mainly in blank verse.

This poem should finally confute those foreign critics who try to fit Lorca into the traditional black legend of Spain: that it is all blood, lust, mysticism and death. The second movement is called 'The blood spilt'; but the whole burden of it is 'No! I won't *look* at it!' The last movement is not an apotheosis, for the dead man's soul is absent. It is a poem difficult to judge on its own merits, for it is inevitably confused in one's mind with the poet's own death a year later: dragged out and shot by some blundering adherents of General Franco.[20] Lorca's poetry remains, in his own words, 'a conscious rocket of dark light, let off among the dull and torpid': *un cohete inteligente de luz oscura en la tonta modorra de las gentes.*

NOTES

[1] The title of a poem by Soto de Rojas (1652). The Granada of this chapter should be compared with the Granada of to-day, described by Mr. Gerald Brenan in *The Face of Spain* (1950).

[2] 'Lo hago para que la gente me quiera; nada más que para me quieran las gentes he hecho ni teatro y mis versos, y seguiré haciéndolos porque es preciso el amor de todos.' *Poema del cante jondo*, 2 ed. Madrid (1937), 146; said to Alfredo Mario Ferreiro in Montevideo.

[3] *Oxford Book of Spanish Verse*, 2 ed., No. 251.

[4] Idem, No. 250.

[5] *Obras completas*, Ed. Guillermo de Torre (Buenos Aires, 1938–48), VII, 122: Las nanas infantiles. An 'omnibus' edition, preface by Jorge Guillén, appeared in 1954. 'El hombre' Alfonso Reyes had said, 'sólo quiere oír lo que sus abuelos contaban; y los narradores de historias buscan el Arte Poética en los labios de la nodriza', *El descastado* (1916).

[6] Idem., VII, 126.

[7] *Oxford Book*, Nos. 249, 250.

[8] *Obras completas*, II, 95. Balada de la placeta, his first published poem.

[9] Idem., II, 65: Balada de un día de julio.

[10] The disinfection, however, must be done with care. 'All words', a correspondent wrote—words as used in poetry—'are boats laden almost down to the water-line with suggestions—and if they are English words they must necessarily carry a cargo of English suggestions; and if you throw them overboard you have a barren, unevocative, prose kind of a word.'

[11] Odes, IV, xiv, 25: Trachiniae, 10–14.

[12] It has been observed that this passage in Lorca's *Imagen poética de Góngora* is not far from Valéry in *Eupalinos ou l'architecte*. That Lorca had Valéry in mind is probable, because he mentions him by name; and he was at the Residencia in 1924 when Valéry came there to lecture.

[13] *Oxford Book*, No. 247. The translations were made for a friend twenty-five or thrity years ago, when the poems were new and no one had thought of putting them into English; but the sense is a poor substitute for the sound.

[14] *Obras completas*, IV, 102.

[15] *Oxford Book*, No. 246.

[16] Gerardo Diego, *Poesía española . . . contemporáneos* (1931), p. 298; (1934), p. 423.

[17] The Spanish *duende* has generally been identified with the Latin DOMITUS, house-spirit; but see the article by Yakov Malkiel in *Estudios Hispánicos: Homenaje a Archer M. Huntingdon*, Wellesley, Mass. (1952), 361–392. Alfonso Reyes speaks somewhere of 'la hora del duende' and we may remember Calderón's play, *La dama duende*, referred to in Chapter VII.

[18] *Obras completas*, VII, 142–143.

[19] One of the critics who was present at the first performance of *Yerma* has written to me as follows:

'La Argentinita, la noche del estreno de *Yerma*, nos decía esto: "La obra es la propia tragedia de Federico. A él lo que más le gustaría en este mundo es quedar embarazado y parir . . . Es ello lo que verdaderamente echa de menos: estar preñado, dar a luz un niño o una niña . . . Yo creo que lo que más le gustaría sería un niño . . . Yerma es Federico, la tragedia de Federico".'

[20] Brenan, t.c., 127–148. See also, Marie Laffrangue, *Textes en prose tirés de l'oubli*. Bordeaux: Bull. Hisp. LVI, No. 3 (1954).

II

UNAMUNO

I

UNAMUNO always said that he disliked music. That is not a criticism of him, but a statement of fact. Like many of his other likes and dislikes, the reason was philological; for that was the way his mind worked. In Spanish, *música celestial* has come to mean 'complete nonsense'; and a chance remark ¡ *Eso es música*! overheard in the street, conveyed a sense of scorn greater than might have been imagined. For Unamuno, when a word had come to mean anything, the word *was* that thing. The word *música* was used for nonsense, therefore music *was* nonsense.

If anyone had dared to tell him that music had been defined as the art of reasoning in sound (*l'art de penser avec les sons*) he would have thought it a frivolous and unseemly paradox; and he would have been distinctly nettled, if he thought that his work could have been compared with a composer's. I like to think of it in three periods; and though in my own private mythology three periods inevitably suggest Beethoven, there is no reason why they should suggest Beethoven to anyone else. The lives of most creators fall into three periods, unless they live long enough to have a fourth period; and Unamuno, when he died at the end of 1936, had achieved the respectable but not extravagant age of 72.

Unamuno wrote essays and poems, novels, short stories and plays; he occupied his mind with philosophy, theology, sociology (how he hated the word!), language and landscape. But, like Beethoven who all his life was writing sonatas, Unamuno, first and last, was a writer of essays. He was Professor Greek in the University of Salamanca; yet he never, so far as I know, published any contribution to classical studies. He certainly meant to. In a letter to Rubén Darío, written in 1899, he says that he hopes one day to publish his ideas of Greek literature,

a result of my professorship, and of the constant influence on my mind—which actually is not very Greek—of that literature which I have been translating and expounding with delight for eight years. Greek has many things in it, and many different things; I shall develop my ideas on it in my study of the gigantic figure of Aeschylus.[1]

24

He never did so; though there was an essay, or perhaps a Platonic dialogue, *Eróstrato o la gloria*: that Erostratus who wished to be remembered for setting fire to the temple of Diana at Ephesus. It was announced in 1902 but seems never to have been printed. We may wonder what prevented him. His position at Salamanca, it is true, was not very like that of a University Professor in a humane subject in England or Scotland; it was more like that of a school-master in charge of a lower form, and his pupils were generally beginners. Men who once sat under him have said that he made them construe literally, gave a few grammatical explanations, and then dictated a translation of his own. Yet he pushed them on, and in their second year they were reading Aeschylus' *Prometheus Vinctus*. Some of us can remember masters who did the same; but they were often well-known scholars who edited the annotated texts we used in school, and contributed learned articles to the *Classical Review* or Latin verses to the *Westminster Gazette*. Unamuno's essays show that he was reasonably well-read in the classics; better in Latin, perhaps, than in Greek. He never over-whelms the reader with classical quotations, but the quotation when it comes is always appropriate. Rubén Darío considered that 'his conscientious "frequentation" of the classics in all languages had given his poetical expression a certain rigidity';[2] but he was less rigid than some classical scholars of his time, for he could tolerate New Testament Greek alongside of Plato and Aeschylus, and towards the end of his life he used to read an Athenian daily paper, Ἐλευθέρον Βῆμα from which he said he got a good many ideas and even some turns of phrase. In Latin, he preferred Lucan to Virgil. The reason was not linguistic but temperamental. Lucan, with his passionate, moral attitude to politics, looked not only Roman but Spanish—it is one of the qualities which the Spaniards of to-day share with the Romans of Lucan's time—while Virgil seemed to him 'feminine'. That shows a certain insensitiveness in Unamuno; or perhaps it was the result of bad teaching at school. 'Like salt on the sweetness of the "Swan of Mantua" such memories brought back to me the torments of the dictionary, and sleepless nights full of gerunds and dactyls and spondees and other ugly things.'[3]

Another of Unamuno's reasons for never publishing anything on classical scholarship was his isolation; not many classical periodicals can have reached Salamanca in those days, and he can hardly have been well informed of what other scholars were doing. By 1906 he had lost interest in it. 'The greatest praise I can think of,

for Greek literature, is to say that, in the fifteen years I have been
teaching the language, the classics have only confirmed the profound
anti-hellenism of my mind, although tempering it to a certain
extent.'⁴ His Basque origin may have had something to do with it;
but what a difference there is between him and his Catalan contemporaries working from the Mediterranean! There was the poet
Maragall writing his *Nausica* and turning the Homeric hymns into
Catalan from a literal translation by Bosch Gimpera; Segala,
Professor of Greek in the University of Barcelona, working on
Attic inscriptions, and Nicolau d'Olwer on the fragments of
Menander; Carles Riba, making a translation of the Odyssey, and
then doing a different one because he was not happy with the first;
and lastly, the editors and translators of the Greek and Latin texts of
the 'Fundació Bernat Metge', the Catalan equivalent of the 'Association Guillaume Budé' and the 'Loeb Classics'.

Yet another reason for Unamuno's failing interest in Greek was
the variety of his interests. He had taught himself to read several
modern languages, though as far as speaking went they were—
and remained—dead languages. French, of course. 'I can clothe my
thoughts in French', he said at Cambridge in 1936, 'but I can only
strip them naked in Castilian' (*yo les dije algunas palabras en francés,
pero no tantas; pues aunque sé revestir mis pensamientos en francés,
sólo sé desnudarlos en castellano*). He read Italian for its poets,
Dante, Leopardi and Carducci; German for its philosophers and
protestant theologians; Danish for Ibsen and Kierkegaard whom
he was reading as early as 1900; English for its literature and thought
in general, with which he was startlingly well acquainted. 'Mis
preferencias van siempre por lo inglés', he wrote to Maragall in
1906, while to Rubén Darío he confessed that he preferred 'the
musings of Browning' to all the French symbolists. He had a
large collection of English books, new and old; they had been carefully read and were full of pencil-marks. He enjoyed the visits of
young Englishmen: Crawford Flitch, Lyulph Howard, and the
American Royall Tyler. 'I have spent years', he wrote in 1911,
'studying philology and teaching it from my Chair; I have spent
years in the study of philosophy and religion and other things; but
it has never occurred to me to publish any work which claimed
to be scientific or a work of scholarship. All my books, good or
bad, are literary or imaginative; poetic, if you like. I don't like
deception. I fish without bait; anyone who likes can bite.'⁵ The
worst of it is that most of those who study Unamuno do fish with

bait, and so catch the kind of fish they expect. It is more profitable to use a landing-net.

A last reason for Unamuno's neglect of classical scholarship was the inadequacy of his professorial stipend. He was the father of a family, and had begun to find that Spanish papers—especially *El Imparcial* of Madrid (which had a Monday Literary Supplement, *Lunes del Imparcial*)—were always ready to print his articles. Rubén Darío seems to have introduced him to *La Nación* of Buenos Aires, and he is pleasantly surprised to find how well they pay: three times as much as they do in Madrid.[6] *La Nación* was suppressed by a recent Argentine dictatorship; but in Unamuno's time it had already a great literary tradition. It had made the reputation of Rubén Darío; it allowed more space than any paper in Spain, and was prepared to print contributions which were not mere newspaper articles, but literary essays in the English sense. 'Unamuno's essays', Rubén Darío said, are *ensayos a la inglesa escritos a la unamunesco*.[7]

2

From the beginning, then, Unamuno wrote essays: articles which were more carefully written, and more forcefully written, than those of his contemporaries. In 1889 he began his first novel, *Paz en la guerra*; but it took eight years to write, and meanwhile he produced the five essays called *En torno al casticismo* (about 'Spanishness'). They were published in a magazine, *La España Moderna*, from February to June 1895, though not collected into a book until 1902. The dates are interesting. These essays which now seem so full of familiar things about the Castilian scene, the Castilian spirit, and the rise and fulfilment of the Spanish genius, were published before any other writings of the kind: before Ganivet's *Idearium Español* (1897), and before the Spanish-American war which led to the literary revival of 'the generation of 1898'. Unamuno afterwards wished[8] that he could have read the *genialísimo* Ganivet first; but he also claimed[9] that his influence on Ganivet had been greater than Ganivet's influence on him. In a letter to Leopoldo Alas (1900) he regretted that that good novelist but captious critic had given so little importance to *el brioso y originalísimo Ganivet*.[10] Unamuno and Ganivet had first met when they were candidates together for Greek lectureships in 1891.

Unamuno introduces the physical geography and climate of Castille in paragraphs which have never been bettered, and then goes on to a masterly examination of the 'climate of opinion' shown in the writings of various periods: the early legal code of the *Fuero Juzgo*, the Poem of the Cid, *Don Quixote* and Quevedo, Santa Teresa and the lesser devotional writers. Other books of the time added points. Salillas' *Hampa* (1898) gave an account of the social conditions which produced the realistic Renascence 'picaresque' novel and the restless Castilian spirit. Poverty of the soil and the meagre basis of subsistence were the chief causes which drove so many able-bodied men to be fugitives and vagabonds.

Then Unamuno hit on the differences caused in peoples by whether they have once been, in their earlier stages, farm-labourers or shepherds; and he began to see how much could be learnt about Castilian psychology from that point of view. It was the old story of Cain and Abel. Abel was a keeper of sheep, and Cain a tiller of the ground. The first crime was fratricide: the murder of a wandering shepherd by his brother who was a sedentary cultivator; and then the sons of Cain were banished to the land of Nod and founded the first town, Enoch. This story haunted Unamuno throughout his life; it also haunted Antonio Machado, and later it came to haunt Dame Edith Sitwell. There are some curious things about it. One is that it puts, right at the beginning of history, the hatred of the sedentary farmworker for the shepherd; another, that it attributes the first murder, not to the struggle for existence, but to envy.[11]

Unamuno may have read in Homer of the struggle of the Lapithae who lived on the fertile river-plains of Peneus in Thessaly, with the 'mountain-haunting' Centaurs of Mount Pelion. Men with a double home, the mountain-haunters moved backwards and forwards between the highlands and the plains, a permanent menace to their sedentary neighbours, the Lapithae. In Homer the sedentary Lapithae won, and in Spain the Moslems won, at first. But in later Greek history the Centaurs became the rough shepherds, robbers and Klefts,[12] with their ballads full of the victorious fight for independence, and the Castilians triumphed over the Moslems in the same way. Popular sympathy always lay with the mountaineer or the man on a horse. The Book of Genesis puts it in another way when it tells how the Lord had more respect for the keeper of sheep than for the tiller of the ground; and this seems to be confirmed in the history of the Spanish peoples. The keeper of sheep became the cattle-man on a horse, the *caballero*; the tiller of the ground became the townsman, the merchant, whom the *caballero* treated as an inferior. Then, in Castille, the poverty of the soil, compared with some other parts of Spain, drove the inhabitants to pasture rather than cultivation; and the pasturing was, to a large extent, that of the migratory shepherds.

At the beginning of June and the end of September (Unamuno noted) we were always woken up one morning by the bleating of the merino sheep which stopped for a rest in front of our house at Salamanca, on the old *cañada real* (the royal cattle track).

The story of the *cañadas* and the sheep driven along them for the Breeders' Association, the *Consejo de la Mesta* to which all other interests had to give way, goes to the root of the conflict between shepherds and farm-workers, and is of the first importance for any real understanding of the history of Spain. It is fully described by Julius Klein in *The Mesta* (Harvard Economic Series) and admirably summarized in *The Spanish Labyrinth* by Gerald Brenan. An earlier English book, *The Spanish People* by Martin Hume, (reviewed by Unamuno) put it in a nutshell by saying that 'the pure Spaniard (i.e. the Castilian) continued, as he had always been, an agriculturist by necessity and a shepherd by choice, when he was not a soldier'.

Unamuno saw, too, how the man who by evocation, tradition and inheritance was a migratory shepherd became an adventurer or a *conquistador* in the Spanish 'Indies' in America, rather than stay at home and till the soil. The greater number of those who went to America were, like Cortés and Pizarro, men from pastures rather than from plough-land or market-gardens. He also realized— few others have done so—that the hatred of Castilians for the 'Moors' (Moslems) in Spain came from reasons which were not so much religious as economic: the *Reconquista* of Spain from Islam was, in fact, the revenge of the sons of Abel on the descendants of Cain, the revenge of the Centaurs on the Lapithae, of migratory shepherds on sedentary cultivators.

These five essays of Unamuno on *casticismo* sowed the seeds of the large literature on the subject which has grown up since 1898; and also, unfortunately, of all the clichés and vulgarisms about Castille and Castilians, with the empty words about *hispanidad* which are exploited by writers to-day. Yet Unamuno was only a Castilian by adoption. By birth he was a Basque; and the novel on which he had been working for so long was an intimate study— an *intra-historia* he called it—of the Second Carlist war in the 'seventies of the last century and the siege and bombardment of Bilbao which he went through as a boy. *Paz en la guerra* was not to be Unamuno's only novel, nor is it a conventional novel; but in one sense it is more like an ordinary novel than his later attempts. There are studies of country people whom he had seen or known, set in their usual scenery and acting and talking the second Carlist war as he remembered people acting and talking it when he was a boy; and the chapters are like essays run together to form a novel of his own youth. Afterwards he treated his material differently, used the ingredients separately. The later novels have no scenery; they might be happening anywhere, in any part of Spain, at any time during Unamuno's life. Descriptions are deliberately avoided in order to achieve 'the greatest intensity and the most dramatic quality'. Landscape is kept for separate essays.

The writings of Unamuno's first period have a feeling of adventure, an assumption of confidence hiding an uncertainty whether the effect on the reader will follow; there is always the need to say something startling to attract and hold the attention. Unamuno himself was aware of this: *tratábase de llamar la atención del público*, he said. He was not the first person to do so; once more there is Beethoven beginning with a loud, decided musical phrase to make the audience sit up and stop talking. At that particular moment in the history of Spain it was necessary to attract attention. Before 1898 there had been a sense of uselessness and frustration, shown in the last essay of *En torno al casticismo*. Then came the loss of the last remaining colonies: Cuba, Puerto Rico and the Philippines; and the younger writers reacted with the vigour which we find in the suppressed prologue to Unamuno's essays.

Unamuno's best-known books belong to his second period. The one which, to my mind, has most clearly 'dated' is the *Vida de Don Quixote y Sancho* (1905). Unamuno belonged to that school of criticism which believed that Don Quixote and Hamlet were far above the writers who created them, and had come into the world without the authors knowing how or why. That view is a thing of the past. For us to-day, the figure of Don Quixote remains as high as ever it was—however it may have been vulgarized by films, distorted by broadcasts, or used for political propaganda; the only modern version which one can respect is the Vic-Wells ballet contrived by Madame Ninette de Valois with music by Roberto Gerhard, and Dulcinea danced by Margot Fonteyn. The figure of Cervantes, however, has acquired a sympathy and humanity which it never had before. That kindly, tolerant, disillusioned, undictatorial man, who could mean more than one thing at a time and still leave us guessing how the humour came in—that is the kind of man we most want to-day—to show the absurdity of our extremisms and lead us gently on the road to a new Age of Reason.

A man like that was not for Unamuno, who had little sense of humour or appreciation of the graces of life, and was himself not a Cervantes but a Quixote. So Antonio Machado saw him in a well-known poem

> Este donquijotesco
> Don Miguel de Unamuno,

who worked to awaken the un-souled soul, the *alma desalmada*, of his country. In his 'Life' of Don Quixote and Sancho he tried to deliver them from what he took for misunderstandings and frivolities on the part of Cervantes, who, after all, had invented both of them. Cervantes might have invented Unamuno, too. Unamuno was, in fact, the village recluse, *el solitario de la aldea*; the type which, in a village in La Mancha, became Don Quixote, but in the University of Salamanca became Don Miguel de Unamuno.

The typical book of Unamuno's second period is *El sentimiento trágico de la vida* (1913). It is his most famous work and one again in which anyone can fish to see what he can catch; though people who fish with orthodox bait will sometimes get bites which surprise them. It, too, is a book of essays begun at least ten years before under different names, so he told Maragall. 'These essays', he says at the end, 'have been going from my hands to the printer's in a sort of improvisation, on notes taken over several years.' Far from constructing a reasoned argument in philosophy or theology, he declares that when writing one essay, he never had before him those that were already written. So they are full of contradictions—apparent contradictions, at any rate—like life or like Unamuno himself.

To a certain extent the book is about death. Unamuno did not fear death, but annihilation. That view is put forcibly in some of his sonnets. Death is *Aquella* ('That Thing') or *La Intrusa* ('The Intruder'); and one can only defend oneself by dreaming, or by hiding one's head, like a child in its mother's lap, or by holding firmly to 'that absurd, illusory belief which is life'. The tragedy of 'The Tragic Sense of Life' is not death, but loss of faith; loss of the sense of personal, individual immortality.

HINC INDIGNATUR SE MORTALEM ESSE CREATUM

Extinction! An individualist like Unamuno could not face that. He could not bear the thought of Lucretius, apparently confronting annihilation without a tremor. 'That terrible poet', he calls him; yet Lucretius' sombre, magnificent line

MORTALEM VITAM MORS CUM IMMORTALIS ADEMIT

echoes at the end of one of Unamuno's most striking sonnets:

una muerte inmortal como corona.

And so, though protesting passionately against loss of faith, Unamuno felt it his duty to knock holes in blind acceptance of faith: 'the faith of a coal-heaver'.[13] He also attacked the indifferent: the people who said 'yes' as well as those who said 'no', and those who would not commit themselves; he was against all those who resigned themselves without a struggle to catholicism, rationalism or agnosticism. The mind, he said, should always be on the alert for something new.[14]

No wonder the Church disapproved! Churchmen came to see him, to dispute with him; but he had read too much theology to be convinced by their arguments. He knew the mind of Catholic Spain; we see it in the poem *El Cristo de Velázquez*. But he knew, too, what Catholics were thinking outside Spain, and he read the Protestant theologians also—a crime for which, in earlier times, he would certainly have been put out of the way by the Holy Inquisition.

Spaniards he thought fundamentally religious, 'whether we know it or not, whether we like it or not'; and though some of them might think themselves rationalists or atheists, the most important problem in their education was to form a clear idea of that subconscious, popular religiosity.

That is what I have been trying to do in this book. . . . What I call the tragic sense of life is, in the end, our own tragic sense of life: that of Spaniards and Spanish people generally, such as is reflected in my own consciousness, which is a Spanish consciousness, made in Spain . . . Spanish religion, like much else, is popular, and also tragic . . . So I have tried in these essays to show the soul of a Spaniard, and in that soul the soul of Spain.

3

Unamuno's contribution to Spanish thought was not only in philosophy and theology, but in poetry compounded of the land-

scape, language and history of Spain; and of Portugal, too, for which
Unamuno had great sympathy and understanding.[15] That relation
is found chiefly in the essays of the second period: *Por tierras de
Portugal y de España* (we notice that Portugal is put first) and
Andanzas y visiones españolas; but it is implicit in the essays published
at the beginning of his career: *Paisajes* (1902) and *De mi país* (1903),
as well as in his correspondence with Maragall and the essays of his
third period when he was banished by the dictatorship of Primo de
Rivera, and again on his return after the proclamation of the Second
Republic in 1931. They are *paisajes de alma*, landscapes of the mind
or soul. The linguistic and historical feeling for landscape is there,
too, in many of the sonnets and other poems, and even in some of
the essays in which, in their way, are poems also. Landscape, he
says, is a language, and language is landscape. We should try to
contemplate nature as history, and history as nature; and in most of
the essays collected since his death—and particularly in *La ciudad
de Henoc, Cuenca ibérica* and *La enormidad de España*, printed in Mexico
between 1941 and 1945—language, landscape and history are tightly
interlaced.

The value of Unamuno's interpretation of landscape has not
escaped the commentators; but the linguistic side of it has not been
properly appreciated. As a linguist—in the strict sense of the word—
Unamuno may have been rather old-fashioned. He belonged more
to the age of Max Müller; yet he had a sense of the poetry and
philosophy of the language of Spain which is most instructive.
Unamuno tried to get to the root of things through the Spanish
words for them. Kant had talked of the thing in itself. 'No', said
Unamuno, 'the *name* in itself! Names are souls of things.'[16] (We
find the same idea in a poem of Juan Ramón Jiménez, *Intelijencia*,
published in 1916.) They had accused Unamuno of *discurrir
imaginativamente con el lenguaje*.[17] And why not? What could be
better? And he might have added, with Sancho Panza, *¿Otro
reprochador de voquibles tenemos?*

On the other side, Unamuno had read enough Wordsworth
to know that his attitude to landscape depended on the emotion
caused in himself by contemplating it. 'I can only appreciate
nature by the impression it produces on me', he had written, as
long ago as 1885; and he told Rubén Darío in a letter that no French
poet had impressed him so profoundly as Wordsworth.[18] It was

the contemplation of nature which had kept him going after the disaster of 1898.

And that's why I isolate myself in this little corner (Salamanca) and don't ever want to leave it. Here in my house, facing the balcony, I have the whole of the Sierra de Gredos—covered with snow just now—and that's a whole universe for me.[19]

No wonder Rubén Darío told people that Unamuno was above all things a poet: *ante todo un poeta y quizá sólo eso*.[20] If being a poet is 'to lean out of the gates of mystery and came back with a glint of the unknown in your eyes', then Unamuno was certainly a poet. 'His vision of the universe is full of poetry. He is the pelota-player of the Apocalypse: *un pelotari de Patmos*',[21] playing his Basque games on the island of St. John the Divine. And yet, in spite of that, Rubén Darío noticed a certain northern air about him, which made some of his poems look 'as if they had been translated from poets with blue eyes'.[22]

The greatest poetic experience in Unamuno's life was the Sierra de Gredos. The most memorable of the *Andanzas y visiones* records an expedition to Gredos, described in the closely-knit, confident prose of the second period; but here the second period is not enough, and we cannot form an idea of what Gredos meant to Unamuno without completing the account of the expedition in the *Andanzas* from the later essays and sonnets written in exile at Fuerteventura or in Paris. The daily vision of Gredos from his balcony, and the hard going of his various attempts to climb it, had become part of his being; but the emotion only became poetry when recollected . . . not in tranquillity, but in the longing to be back again at Salamanca.

> No, no es Gredos aquella cordillera;

'No, that's not Gredos, that low line of hills', he exclaimed in his back bedroom at Hendaye, in the little hotel opposite the railway station, gazing at the Pyrenees over the frontier which he might not cross. On Gredos, the highest peak is named Almanzor after the great prime minister of the Spanish caliph of Córdoba, and in the 'silence of the ever-open jaws of heaven, there Almanzor's great finger points, and sets his seal; but, as he passes by, taps with his nail and those mock mountains break'.

> ¡ Aquel silencio de la inmensa boca
> del cielo, en que ponía sello el dedo
> del Almanzor ! ¡ En su uña al paso choca
> y se rompe la sierra de remedo !

Then there was the memory of the straight, sunny Zamora road, once a daily walk at Salamanca, 'the daily round of all my happiest dreams'.

> ¡ Oh, clara carretera de Zamora,
> soñadero feliz de mi costumbre . . .!

But now he saw it through a criss-cross of boulevards, *esquares*, avenues and the sewer-like entrances to the Paris Métro.

When I was nearly sixty (he wrote in an autobiographical sonnet on his banishment) my destiny—the one I left behind in my native town—rose from the depths of dream and blindingly flashed a new future right across my path. The might-have-been, the life my lot had smothered in a professor's chair in Old Castille, came back to me again across the sea, bringing me bright new flax and a new distaff. To be at last, what I had dreamed, a poet. . . .

> Hacerme, al fin, el que soñé, poeta . . .

One more sonnet. I still hear him reading it in the little room at Hendaye. He hated declamation. His poems were really meant, I think, to be read silently. They were for sessions of silent thought; and unless the language ran away with him, he made a poem sound as much as possible like prose. In spite of that, he could make it burn and crackle like Moses' burning bush.

> '¡ Miguel ! ¡ Miguel !' 'Aquí, Señor, desnudo
> me tienes a tu pie.'
> The Voice: 'Miguel, Miguel !' 'Lord, here am I, Naked before thy feet.' [23]

It is the sonnet on hearing the voice of God—the Old Testament God of Spain who has his throne in the Sierra de Gredos. Unamuno, with his intense individualism, had made God (as he had made Paris) in his own image. He was a holy and humble man of heart, no doubt; but no man ever took more pride in his humility. In his presence one felt like a worm in the presence of a prophet—a prophet like Isaiah, who was also a poet.

All through life he had a habit of making birds of folded paper; but by the time he was sixty, the birds had got into his poetry and the poetry into the birds. One day a small boy asked him if a paper bird could talk, and he made it talk in its paper voice—in verse: a mixture of poetry and theology, which a friend has translated:

> Talk. The child wants you to talk.
> And the bird speaks: Hark !
> The Son of Man,
> flesh of the word,
> was in the cradle

made God,
to a song of children
of the wood,
a song with wings,
a bird.
Talk.   The child wants you to talk.
Paper voice, paper bird,
talk to the child!
he has heard
the voice descending
ending—and then a hush—
over the marsh.
The child is alive:
his heart is filled
with the growing God.
Talk to the child.
You are the dove
of Pentecost
whose hand made man:
the Holy Ghost.
Talk to the children:
the kingdom of heaven
and all the dreams
to a child are given.
A child, king
of the dreams we had.
A child, heart
of all things made.
Talk.   The child wants you to talk.
And the bird   speaks: hark![24]

Many of the sonnets are really essays: essays in little, with the blend of landscape, language and history that we find in the essays too. But it seems to have escaped the commentators that while many of the sonnets are really essays, many of the essays are really poems. I do not mean the poems included in the *Andanzas y visiones*; poems which are printed as poems, or the pieces which are halfway between prose and verse.

It may be (Unamuno wrote) that only music can express the most intimate part of a landscape: its sense of rhythm. But I, though I may be something of a poet—and a lunatic—am less than nothing of a musician. Still, my sense of rhythm (which must be musical to a certain extent)—the rhythm of the country and the things one sees there—has not always fitted completely into prose, and sometimes I have turned it into verse.[25]

Prose or verse, some of the essays have a peculiar quality of poetry about them, a quality which reminds one of the odes in pseudo-classical metres—the *Odi Barbare*—of the great Italian poet

Carducci. Unamuno had never known Carducci personally; but he knew his poetry very well indeed—as well as he knew the poetry of Leopardi—and not only the *Odi Barbare*.

Most well-read people of Unamuno's time knew the poems of Carducci; it was only after the 1914 war that he began to drop out, and those who had not read him said that he was old-fashioned. Unamuno wrote a few poems which on paper look like the odes in Sapphic or Asclepiad metres in Horace, though actually every line is a Spanish verse. There is a fine ode to Salamanca, 'a classical form for a classical subject', he told Rubén Darío. As a matter of fact, though the stanzas all end in the regular jingle of the short Adonic line, not one of the other, longer, 11-syllable lines is a Sapphic that Sappho herself would have recognized. Swinburne could imitate it, when he

> Saw the white implacable Aphrodite;

and there are, as it happens, one or two lines in Shakespeare's sonnets which may be read like Greek Sapphics, for instance:

> Thus have I had thee as a dream doth flatter . . .

The Latin Sapphic, however, was different; for the Roman poets lengthened the fourth syllable, and generally divided their lines after the fifth. Unamuno never saw the white implacable Aphrodite; but his ode to Salamanca and to the Tower of Monterrey—which was just up the street from his own house—are fine poems.

The likeness to Carducci comes out in those passages in the essays which are a poetical bird's eye view of history—history seen from the particular point of view of a certain object: a fountain, a river, a buried statue of Victory, or the two leaning towers of Bologna and the things they have seen going on beneath them.

These are the subjects of some of Carducci's *Odi Barbare*, and it is not difficult to find examples—in prose—in the essays of Unamuno. The best is in one of the later essays, reprinted in the Mexican collection *Cuenca ibérica*, and in *Paisajes del alma* published at Madrid. The essay is called *Los delfines de Santa Brígida*, and conjures up the history of Spain since the end of the eighteenth century, seen by the two dolphins on a fountain in Madrid:

Carlos IV, María Luisa, Godoy, Goya. The eve of the Revolution—the French one—and the splashings, overflowings, and repercussions which the dolphins afterwards felt, without ever ceasing to pour out their fresh water—symbolic dolphins!

And then Napoleon and the revolt of the *Dos de Mayo*—and the guns at Monteleón—when some of those Goyesque figures came to quench in the waters of

St. Brigit the thirst that came of street-fighting. And then Ferdinand VII, *el deseado*, so desired by the water-carriers who bawled rude remarks after him.

And the dolphins heard the Republican National Anthem, the Hymn of Riego, who was afterwards carried to execution in a crate. And they heard news of the first Carlists, when Gómez reached the outskirts of Madrid. And they heard the footsteps of the other Revolution, our own, the September Revolution, which carried off Isabel II; and there was General Prim . . . and in the distance the bang of the blunderbuss which did him in.

The Second Carlist War came, the one Unamuno saw himself.

And meanwhile every year—and there are now a hunded and sixty of them—the enturtled dolphins heard on the feast of St. Anthony a sound of hoofs and neighing and braying and grunting, and the shouts of horsemen, and people on foot. For horses came by, and mules—some harnessed like a *maja* in her best; asses, she-asses, pack-mules and pigs . . . and all to have their fodder blessed! And there's also the blessing of the fields, so that the dolphins in the sky may give us the rain that brings hay and grapes and olives; and corn which gives us our daily bread, while it tightens our belts when we think of our history.

That is Unamuno in his third period: something which begins like Carducci at Clitumnus and ends like Charles Kingsley in *The Water Babies*.

4

Unamuno never forgot his boyish experience of civil war. He even believed in war—or said that he did, from love of paradox— even in 1920 after the first world war, when it seemed clear to some of his visitors that there need never have been a war at all. While things were blowing up for another war in Spain, from 1933 to 1936, he could not keep silent. Rashly, but from a sense of duty, he allowed himself to be elected to the Cortes Constituyentes; but he was too quick-witted, too hasty, too little able to suffer fools gladly, to tolerate constitution-making and government by discussion, when eight years of dictatorship had made most of the legislators forget what government by discussion really meant. He never realized that one of the minor horrors of war is that speaking your mind is impossible; and when finally, in July 1936, the military leaders attacked the government, Unamuno said things which made some people think that he had gone in with the rebels. But if anyone thought, from his paradoxical sayings and his bitter tongue, that he had joined the military revolt, they were soon undeceived. Unamuno had never lacked courage, and the war had caught him in Salamanca which was a rebel stronghold. At a public meeting on October 12th, Columbus Day (*el día de la raza*) he told the generals—the *militarotes*—exactly what he thought of them. 'You can win' (*vencer*) he said, 'but you can never convince' (*convencer*), and he was never allowed to leave his house again.[26]

The man who knew most about the last days of Unamuno was a Dutch professor, Dr. Brouwer, a Roman Catholic who was afterwards shot by the Nazis in Holland. In the autumn of 1936 he made his way into the rebel zone of Spain, and at last saw Unamuno at Salamanca. Among those present at the meeting in October had been a screaming scarlet general, a thrice-battered veteran of the wars in Morocco, whose crippled condition would have excited pity if his character had been more human. He made a speech, barking at the Catalans and the Basques and all Spaniards who were not Castilians; they had never contributed anything to Spanish history, he declared; creative effort had come from Castille, and from Castille alone. Death to intelligence! Unamuno could contain himself no longer. All his life long he had expounded the greatness of Castille, in essays, poems, philosophy and theology; yet he had always found a place, an indispensable place, for Basques and Catalans and also for the Portuguese. 'The Bishop is a Catalan', he flashed. 'I am a Basque on all four sides. I can stand no more! I will not stand more! If what you say were true and Castille alone responsible for the past glory and future prosperity of Spain, then Spain would be like you: one arm, one foot, one eye; mutilated, loathsome!' Unamuno was shut up in his house; and before they had decided what to do with him, it was too late.

I heard the rest of the story in Mexico. Someone was sitting with him in his house, at Salamanca, on a freezing night at the end of December. There was a brazier, and Unamuno was warming his toes at it and talking. He stopped, and the visitor thought that he had gone to sleep. Suddenly he saw that Unamuno's slippers were burning. He was dead.

NOTES

[1] *Archivo de Rubén Darío* (1943), 34.
[2] *La Nación* (Buenos Aires, 1909), reprinted as prologue to Unamuno's *Teresa* (1924), 8.
[3] Prologue to *Alma América: poemas indo-españoles*, J. Santos Chocano (1905).
[4] *Pompeya* (1902), reprinted in *Paisajes del alma* (Madrid, 1944), 29–30; and *Unamuno y Maragall: Epistolario*, 26 (Barcelona, 1951).
[5] *Ensayos*, VII, 203 (Madrid: Residencia de Estudiantes, 1918).
[6] *Archivo de Rubén Dario*, 35.
[7] Prologue to *Teresa*, 6.
[8] Prologue (afterwards suppressed) to the 1902 edition of *En torno al casticismo*.
[9] Introduction to *El porvenir de España* (1912).
[10] *Epistolario a Clarín* (1941), 85.
[11] The idea that anger, hatred and jealousy were conditions necessary for man's development is examined by Sir Arthur Keith in *A new theory of human evolution* (1948).

[12] N. Bachtin, *Introduction to the study of Modern Greek* (1935), 7.

[13] A. Sánchez Barbudo in an excellent article, *La formación del pensamiento de Unamuno* (Hispanic Review, XVIII, 1950, No. 3) believes that there was a time, about 1897, when Unamuno himself was an unbeliever; while P. Corominas (Revista de Catalunya, No. 83, p. 155) thought that Unamuno 'believed that he believed, but did not really believe'. There is no need to bring von Hugel into the question.

Introducing his *novels*, his long short story *San Manuel Bueno* (1931), Unamuno said: 'I am conscious of having put into it the whole of my tragic sense of daily life'. It is the story of a priest who, like Unamuno, can no longer believe all that he is bound to believe, but must keep up the faith of his parishioners so that their lives may appear to have some meaning. He knows that 'one of those *caudillos*' (meaning Lenin) had described religion as the opium of the people; but he accepts this for the truth, adding that people must be given the opium of religion so that they may be able to live, or at least sleep and dream. For the believer, this must be a terrible story. Unamuno thought no other faith possible than catholicism, the traditional faith of Spain; yet he had lost his belief in it. The modern world had no meaning; there was no value in what man had accomplished, and no sense, either, in what was being attempted in Spain to regenerate the country. Don Francisco Giner and Antonio Machado kept their faith in Spain to the last; but Unamuno lost it. (See Ramón Iglesia, *El reaccionarismo de la generación de 98*, in *Cuadernos americanos*, Mexico, VI, 1947, 5.)

[14] *El sentimiento trágico de la vida*, 317.

[15] The Portugal that Unamuno loved was 'Portugal campesino y sencillo, padre del Portugal navegante y heroico'. In his own words:

Un día Ulises dejó la esteva del arado para ir a la guerra, hizo del leño de sus bosques un corvo navío de negra prora, convirtió la esteva en remo y partió a luchar, y rendida Troya volvió a sus lares y de nuevo el remo se hizo esteva, y por las noches, cabe el hogar, contemplando el onduleo de las llamas de fuego que recordaban el vaivén de las olas marinas, contaba a sus hijos y nietos los trances de la guerra y de sus errabundas navegaciones. Así Portugal.

[16] *La enormidad de España* (1945), pp. 68 and 63.

'Por mi parte', he said once when making a gramophone record, 'nada me molesta más que oir decir de alguien que habla como un libro. Prefiero los libros que hablan como hombres, y lo que es menester es que la gente aprenda a leer con los oídos, no con los ojos. La palabra es lo vivo, la palabra es en el principio. En el principio fué el verbo, y acaso en el fin será el verbo también.' And, he added, 'toda la tragedia íntima, que lo es, ha sido luchar con la palabra para sacarle toda la filosofía, toda la religión que lleva implícita, porque una palabra es la esencia de la cosa'.

[17] *La Ciudad de Henoc* (1941), 153.

[18] *Archivo de Rubén Darío*, 34.

[19] Idem., 36. What the Gredos is like to a climber may be seen in an article by John Ormsby (the translator of Cervantes) in *The Alpine Journal*, VI, Aug. 1872–May 1874.

[20] *Teresa*, 3.

[21] Idem., 6.

[22] Idem., 12.

[23] *Oxford Book of Spanish Verse*, No. 209.

[24] Idem., No. 212. Lorca, too, wrote a poem *Pajarita de papel*, printed in his first book, *Libro de poemas* (1921).

[25] *Andanzas y visiones* (1922), 257.

[26] Compare Guillermo de Torre, *Tríptico del sacrificio*, 2nd. ed. (Buenos Aires, 1948). Unamuno's nephew has described him in his last days, confined to his house in Salamanca, 'oyendo resonar los graves y claros ámbitos de sus plazas y calles con el arrastrar de las teutónicas botazas invasoras, viendo su ciudad vuelta cancha de italianos, de coloniales "salvadores de España" y de indígenas señoritos cipayos, el corazón y el peso de las entrañas se le alzarían contra toda la vergüenza que le rodeaba y se le venía encima, ahogándole.' A few days before he died, shut in his room but never left alone, he said: 'De aquí ya no saldré si no es para que me fusilen o para el cementerio': ('I shall never get out of here, except for shooting or the cemetery.') *Hora de España*, XV, Mar. 1938.

For a good selection of Unamuno's prose, see *Prosa diversa*, selected by J. L. Gili (1938). Admirable translations were published by J. E. Crawford Flitch, *Miguel de Unamuno: Essays and Soliloquies* (1925).

The so-called 'complete' editions published in Madrid should be used with caution. Four volumes of uncollected essays have appeared in Buenos Aires, *De esto y de aquello* (1950–53).

III

RUBÉN DARÍO

I

THE *Archivo de Rubén Darío*, the packet of letters to and from the poet published by Alberto Ghiraldo in 1943, must have given many readers a new impression. We had imagined a feckless mixture of Swinburne and Ernest Dowson, a victim of all the conventional Bohemian vices of the 1890's, never able to look after himself, and with no Watts Dunton to make a Putney for him. He turns out to have been a man to whom Unamuno, Antonio Machado and Juan Ramón Jiménez poured out their youthful aspirations and opened their hearts on what they meant to do, one who never failed to be friendly and helpful to people younger than himself. He was always a busy Latin-American journalist and foreign correspondent, often charged with diplomatic missions, and yet a conscious craftsman in prose and verse. 'He always seemed so alive', Juan Ramón Jiménez said, 'so much an equal and yet so distinguished.' He was 'like some rare human monster from the sea, uncouth yet exquisite, more of the sea than of the land'. A seaport (Málaga) or an island (Majorca) suited him best; and from there he would send correspondents bunches of poems; but Madrid made him curl up, like a sea-serpent on dry land. His sea was 'a pagan sea, an elemental sea, with permanent horizons of history and illustrious islands'. Even his poetical technique was maritime. He modelled his verses like waves, and was always inclined to be sea-sick with the wave of Venus or a touch of the sun. 'When he took out his old-fashioned watch, I saw from the taps he gave it, and from his lost look round to the four quarters of the sky, that the thing which enabled him to find his bearings was not a watch but a mariner's compass ... His true country was an island—of the Argonauts or the Cytherean or Columbus. The mainland had no reason for existing other than to be a convenient paradise for all species, divine and human, descended from Venus. His immortality is certain.'

Cuando sacaba su reló anacrónico, yo comprendía, por los golpes que le daba y por su mirar perdido a los cuatro vientos, bocacalles de lo salado imposible, que lo que los orientaba era una brújula: . . . Su patria verdadera fué la isla, de los Argonautas, de Citeres, de Colón . . . Las tierras continentales no tenían otra razón de vida para él que ser paraíso accidental de las especies divinas y humanas descendientes de Venus.

The Majorcan poet, Joan Alcover, whose gentle spirit was disguised by an eye and a beard which might have belonged to a naval officer, described him as *L'hoste*: a Catalan word implying, like the Greek ξένος, a stranger and therefore a guest. 'There came among us a man of intense pallor . . . His name was the echo of cymbals or cockcrow, or the point of a lance that struck on a shield':

> Son nom ens desperta amb la ressonança
> d'un eco de címbal o gall matiner,
> o la punta fina d'un ferro de llança
> qu toca un broquer.

'He came like a rain refreshing the tree of (our) poetry; a new Pygmalion, giving back to the nymph who had turned marble-hearted her life and movement and feeling . . . He passed, and the roses turned redder to see him, and the bubbling spring sang to a deeper note':

> És com una pluja que refresca l'arbre
> de la poesía; nou Pigmalió
> que torna a la nimpha d'entranyes de marbre
> moviment i vida i palpitació . . .
> Quan passa, les roses tornen més vermelles
> i el brollador canta més solemnial.

Catalan poetry owes a debt to him; and he, something to the adventurous, experimental spirit of the Catalonia of his time. It is important to realize that he was neither so ineffectual nor so sensual as is usually believed. If he liked his sea-food with whiskey, if he could never resist a well-turned ankle—all that was visible in those days—if no paradise seemed more certain than a private room in a Parisian restaurant, that was because he was a man of the tropics; and distance lent enchantment, as it did to Bolívar when he talked of the wonders of Paris to his officers in the wilds of Venezuela. Further, Rubén Darío's Paris had the nostalgic and decorative charm of the Paris of Toulouse-Lautrec. His more erotic poems will always make him read, by the young, like Swinburne and San Juan de la Cruz; and, like Swinburne, he explored and developed new possibilities in metre. Like Swinburne, too, he was sensitive to all the winds of political idealism; and his receptive mind caught at new ideas floating round him and turned them into poetry. In that, he was like Carducci and D'Annunzio, who, with Swinburne and Darío himself, were all really of the same family, being ultimately descended from Victor Hugo.

Commentators are apt to forget Rubén Darío's relations with the Italians. He had obviously read Leopardi; he visited Carducci at Bologna in 1905, and returned full of 'barbarous' hexameters; ten years before, he could write of *el verso de fuego de D'Annunzio*. Again his admiration and friendship for the Portuguese symbolist, Eugenio de Castro, form the subject of an essay, with translations, in *Los Raros*. There is one other important connexion: Ovid. Many of his new rhythms were derived from French, Italian and Latin; but we may suspect that he read alexandrines, hexameters and pentameters in his own way and pronounced them with an American Spanish accent. Rubén Darío cannot be explained only from Spanish or French.

With Swinburne and D'Annunzio, 'the thing became a trumpet', as Wordsworth said of the sonnet. But (*The Athenaeum* once remarked) the difficulty is to *prevent* the thing from becoming a trumpet; and the generation after Rubén Darío gave up his alexandrines and hexameters and went back to the old Castilian balladmetre. That damaged his reputation, for it made him look oldfashioned; yet most modern poets speaking Spanish have felt his influence, except Jorge Guillén and Luis Cernuda, and the texture of later Spanish verse is generally finer than it used to be.

Rubén Darío is best known for his public, bard-like utterances, when (like Swinburne) he was 'girdled in his golden singing-coat'. It is from this that later Spanish poets have turned away; but he also had a private manner, one which Spanish had hardly ever heard, even in Bécquer. The quiet poem called *Tarde del trópico*, evening in the tropics, is usually printed in *Cantos de vida y esperanza* (1905); but it was actually written earlier—at sea off Costa Rica in 1892—and printed (under the name of *Sinfonía*) with the declamatory *Canto épico a las glorias de Chile*. That was a prize-poem on the Chilean naval victories over the combined forces of Peru and Bolivia; epic in a medieval sense, like the *Maldon Poem*, the *Chanson de Roland* and the *Siete Infantes de Lara*: the last fight against overwhelming odds of the wooden *Esmeralda* (a Chilean *Revenge*) going down before one of the first ironclads on the Pacific coast, the Peruvian *Huascar*.

Tarde del trópico is the complete opposite: a private poem to be read in a low voice. The evening is grey and sad, the sea clothed in velvet, the deep sky in mourning:

> Es la tarde gris y triste.
> Viste el mar de terciopelo
> y el cielo profundo viste
> de duelo.

From the *abismo*, the abyss—a continuation of the *-is*, in *gris*, *triste*, *viste*, which, with the smoother *-elo* of *terciopelo* (velvet), *cielo* (heaven), *duelo* (grief) has dominated the first stanza, there arises a bitter and sonorous complaint, *amarga y sonora*; the wave, when the wind sings—with the long-drawn syllables in *-nd* and *-nt*— weeps:

> Del abismo se levanta
> la queja amarga y sonora.
> La onda, cuando el viento canta,
> llora.

2

That is an example of Rubén Darío's private manner: something that was new in Spanish. The opposite, the manner for public declamation on themes of urgent public importance, was the hexameter. From a classical point of view these 'hexameters' are only hexameters by courtesy. The question of long and short syllables does not enter, though it is important in some of Rubén Darío's alexandrines. All that is reproduced in the hexameters in the dactylic rhythm and the metrical ictus. The new verses try to be like Homer, but only succeed in being like Longfellow; instead of the Iliad and the Odyssey they recall *Evangeline* and *The Courtship of Miles Standish*.

Actually there were better models for accentual hexameters in Spanish. They are in the *Romancero*, particularly in the later ballads of the *Romancero nuevo* and some of the popular Mexican *corridos*. There is a famous ballad attributed to Lope de Vega:

> Sale la estrella de Venus al tiempo que el sol se pone.

That is a passable accentual hexameter, better than many of Rubén Darío's; and in fact twenty of the forty-four lines of that ballad are hexameters. One of them has a vision of the event as it might have been seen by García Lorca:

> Halló el palacio cubierto de luminarias y voces.

It is curious that Rubén Darío did not think of the Mexican popular ballads, for they, too, sometimes have better and smoother hexameters than his own, for example:

> Dice la niña Rosita, 'Les jugaremos un trato'.

The poem in which Rubén Darío first called to the Spanish-speaking world in accentual hexameters was read aloud one evening at a meeting in Madrid in 1905, and published in *Cantos de vida y esperanza*. This *Salutación del optimista* sounds like a stirring improvization in the style of Walt Whitman. The story is that when the day of the meeting drew near and no lines were written, the poet's friends had to give him more whiskey than usual, and the poem only took shape when he was under its influence. Another account claims that the poem was only written when his friends had succeeded in making him sober; but this sounds an afterthought. Drink did not make him noisy, but merely owl-like, and he is described reading in a way that was slow, solemn and hesitant: *cortada*. The *Salutación del optimista* may not have been written down until the night before; but it had obviously been in the poet's head for some time. It is the challenge of the 'Latin' or 'Iberian' way of life, in Mexico, Central and South America, to what we have now come to call the 'American' way of life, that is, of the North—as if there were only two great, simple patterns in the infinite variety of the American continent!

Rubén Darío realized that when the thing had to become a trumpet—in the depression after the Spanish-American war—the verse to use was the accentual hexameter, or the 14-syllable Spanish alexandrine which could easily be transposed into one. 'A Spaniard of America', he wrote, 'and an American of Spain, I chose for my instrument the Greek and Latin hexameter; and declared my faith and confidence in the resurrection of the ancient Hispania . . . in the chorus of nations which make a balance and counterpoise to the strong, daring race of the North'. He also used hexameters in the poem *A Roosevelt*, to protest against the aggressive intentions and 'dollar-diplomacy' of the first President of that name; and in a later poem, *Los cisnes* (The Swans) dedicated to Juan Ramón Jiménez, he feared that eighty or ninety million Spanish-speaking people might have to give up Spanish and learn English:

> ¿Tantos milliones de hombres hablaremos inglés?

That seemed fantastic until 1940, when it looked as if millions of people speaking English (if they escaped death in a concentration-camp or gas-chamber) would be compelled to learn the Nazi variety of German. If, read to-day, parts of the *Salutación del optimista* sound strangely prophetic, that is due to the poet's sensitive-ness. Rubén Darío was one of the most sensitive poets who ever wrote in Spanish, with delicate antennae and a sixth sense to catch the faintest suggestion of what was going on in people's minds, or what was likely to happen in the world at large. To say in 1905:

Fuertes colosos caen, se desbandan bicéfalas águilas,

and to talk of a *vasto social cataclismo*, was something like a prophesy of the 1914–18 war and its consequences in Austria and Russia.

All this, of course, is rhetoric. The *Salutación del optimista*, like the poem to Roosevelt, are rhetorical poems for rhetorical occasions. Rubén Darío was a Latin poet and not afraid of rhetoric. The poem to King Oscar II of Sweden, *Al rey Oscar*, is more carefully con-sidered. It was inspired by something read in a newspaper. Spain was still in the shadow of 1898, a blow which seemed more deadly than the blow dealt by Bolívar three-quarters of a century before. No one in his senses—outside a government office—would think of war being a good thing or doing anyone any good. But the Spanish-American war was short; there was no invasion or occupa-tion of Spain, and there were men—the generation of 1898—who could learn a lesson from defeat and derive moral and intellectual support from it. With these men, or some of them, Rubén Darío allied himself; and though he missed Don Francisco Giner, the key to the whole movement, he saw that it was not only Spain's great past, but her present human material (though not that of her rulers) which held hope for the future.

Oscar II had the reputation of being somewhat stiff in his own country, and he was unfortunate with Norway. But he was a just and kindly person, more friendly—like many Swedes—when away from his native soil; and when he crossed the Spanish frontier at Irún he exclaimed, from sheer goodness of heart, 'Vive l'Espagne!' In Darío's mind the remark took an importance which the king had probably never given it; and the result was a set of winged, dactylic verses on things which Spain had done in the past and for which she deserved to be remembered. Another political poem, however, *A Colón*, shows how the thought of Spanish-speaking America struck him on a bad day towards the end of 1892, the four-hundredth anniversary of the discovery. 'Unfortunate admiral! Your poor America, the pearl of your dreams, is a hysterical woman, convulsed by nerves and with a dead white face. Oh, that it had pleased God that the waters hitherto untouched had never reflected the white sails; and that the astounded stars had never seen your caravels reach the shore! . . . Christopher Columbus, poor admiral! Pray to God for the world which you discovered!'

> ¡ Plugiera a Dios las aguas antes intactas
> no reflejaran nunca las blancas velas;
> ni vieran las estrellas estupefactas
> arribar a la orilla tus carabelas! . . .
> ¡ Cristóforo Colombo, pobre Almirante,
> ruega a Dios por el mundo que descubriste!

That was a mood which passed. Rubén Darío even came to unsay the things he had said about Theodore Roosevelt. The poem *Salutación al águila* is a versified after-dinner speech which, as delegate for Nicaragua, he made at the Panamerican Congress at Rio in 1906. He was criticized for changing his mind, for giving the opposite view to that expressed in *A Roosevelt*. Yet he meant it; the change of tone was due to his sensitiveness to his surroundings. Many present were obviously sincere in their panamericanism; he would try to convey that sincerity, too, and praise the ideal of the United States. Later, in the *Epístola a la Señora de Leopoldo Lugones* (the wife of his great Argentine contemporary) he said: 'I panamericanized, with a vague fear and little faith . . . But I found, too, a nucleus of cordial souls, full of affection, vision and idealism . . . And then the heat was atrocious!'

How far *A Roosevelt* or *Salutación al águila* are topical to-day might be questioned; but who shall say that the poem immediately following, *A Francia*, is not as topical now, in 1955, as in 1893 when it was written? *Cara Lutecia*, he liked to call the Paris which he loved and understood; and the spirit of the poem is that of George Meredith's on 1870:

> We see a vacant place;
> We hear an iron heel.

3

Rubén Darío was not deeply or widely read in the classics; but when employed in the National Library of Nicaragua he had browsed on a great many books, and had learnt enough Latin to find his way through a good deal of Ovid, and poems once attributed to Ovid like the 'Lament for Drusus', *Epicedion Drusi*, which had inspired part of Garcilaso's first elegy. Reading the poems to himself and scanning them in a Spanish way, he would easily have come upon the strange new effects of rhythm which afterwards dominated his own verse. Verse, he said, was a wing, *ala*, and rhythm a wave, *onda*; he was borne not only on the wings of song (like Goethe and Mendelssohn) but also on the waves of it. In his later verses, though correctly described as alexandrines, we often find something like, or with more than a suggestion of, Latin elegiac couplets: the poem *Los Cisnes*, 'The Swans', for instance. Some of the lines have the rhythm of Latin verses which the poet must have read and remembered (the speech-rhythm, not the metre) and more particularly the speech-rhythm of the pentameter. Rubén Darío and Carducci copied this rhythm in verses which run naturally in their own languages; for instance, a pentameter like the heart-rending line of Propertius, which they would have read:

cum míhi núlla méi sit médicína máli

(since, for me, there may be no medicine for my woe). This appears in Rubén Darío in the form of:

se muéren nuéstras rósas, se agótan nuéstras pálmas.

The elegiac metre suggests the elegiac mood; but Rubén Darío could sometimes achieve the same effect with loose accentual hexameters, and they are among the most beautiful lines he ever wrote:

Bajo tus pies desnudos aún hay blancos de espuma,
y en tus labios compendias la alegría del mundo . . .
Hace una hora que un nombre grabé sobre la nieve;
hace un minuto dije mi amor sobre la arena.

These are smoother and more beautiful in Spanish than the trumpet-toned hexameters of the political poems. They might be pulled to pieces for their prosody: a syllable missing here, no caesura there; and the pundits would be right to call them mere 14-syllabled Spanish alexandrines. But the frequency of the dactylic feet makes the comparison with hexameters inevitable; and it is noteworthy that Alfonso Reyes, in his new and splendid Spanish version of the Iliad, has not hesitated to use alexandrines instead of hexameters.

'The movement of liberation in poetry, which it was my lot to begin in America, spread to Spain', Rubén Darío remarked, with pardonable pride. Actually that was an exaggeration. Rhythmical liberation had already appeared in Mexico, Cuba, Colombia, Argentina, and other South American countries; and in Spain itself— where, he said, 'poetic expression was stiff-jointed, *anquilosada*, to the point that the mummification of rhythm had become an article of faith'. Only the Málaga poet, Salvador Rueda, had been experimenting with alexandrines which could also be read as hexameters.

The poet's sensitiveness is directly related to the quality of his symbolism. We may take the swan, the sphinx and the butterfly. The swan came from Ovid; it drew the chariot of Venus through the air, but was also a disguise for Jupiter when he came down to make love to Leda. As a result of that, Rubén Darío remembered, Leda laid an egg, from which was hatched Helen of Troy.

> Si antes la blanca Helena
> del huevo azul de Leda brotó la gracia llena.

Rubén Darío combined the Ovidian swan with the Wagnerian swan in Lohengrin: 'as if it were a sculptured icicle that moved, with arching neck and formed into an S'.

> Lohengrin; y su cisne, cual si fuese
> un cincelado témpano viajero,
> con su cuello enarcado en forma de S.

Then the swan's arched neck became a question-mark to interrogate the Sphinx

> con la interrogación de su cuello divino.

What was the Sphinx?

With so shy a man who left on all who knew him the impression of a friendly soft-voiced child of nature, unlike anyone else, it is difficult to take literally his boasted virility. A perfervid erotic imagination, first excited by the Song of Solomon, permeated his poetry from the time of an early sonnet to the late *Poema del otoño*; but it was only when middle-aged and prematurely grey in head and heart: *las prematuras canas de alma y cabeza*, that he realized what a Don Juan he might have been. When he was younger he could feel the spring in his veins like D'Annunzio or Don Giovanni:

> Una musica
> magnífica. Una suprema
> inspiración primitiva
> llena de cosas modernas.
> Un vasto orgullo viril
> que aroma el *odor di femmina* . .

But middle age, he found, was 'woven of flesh and perfumed with wine', leading to the mood of hangover when nothing can be enjoyed any more and one does not know what to do next.

> Y esta atroz amargura de no gustar de nada,
> de no saber adónde dirigir nuestra prora.

These were the thoughts behind the sonnet *La dulzura del Angelus*, suggested (Mr. Dundas Craig thinks) by Millet's popular picture. The same is true of the *Canción de Otoño en Primavera*,

> Juventud, divino tesoro,

There are also the verses called *Nocturno* in which he tried to express what would now be called his 'Angst' (*mi angustia*) in verses which would tell of his vanished youth of roses and dreams:

> en versos que abolida
> dirán mi juventud de rosas y de ensueños.

Dreams, of course, but hardly roses. A wandering life of perpetual journalism and writing articles against time, stimulated (and often only made possible) by a little whiskey, had used him up by the time he was forty. Pedro Salinas, in his excellent book, *La poesía de Rubén Darío*, staked too heavily, perhaps, on his sensuality. Still, there is plenty of circumstantial evidence, if the poetry is taken literally (as a French critic has taken Swinburne's) for an account of what actually happened rather than what happened in the poet's imagination. There are hints that the reality of the adventures was more ordinary; though Rubén Darío, like Unamuno and the man of flesh and bones, imagined the Muse to have flesh and bones too:

> La mejor musa es la de carne y hueso

—someone who might be taken out to dinner at a Parisian restaurant; and when he went home to Nicaragua, he saw in every woman, even the brownest Indian, a Greek nymph:

> En cada mujer miro como una ninfa griega.

Psychoanalysis had not been invented, but Rubén Darío knew vaguely what was the matter. He called it *La Esfinge*, *el esfinge interior*, *la enamorada esfinge*, *el feminino arcano*, *un monstruo malhechor llamado Esfinge*; and in his poetry he tried to sublimate it: *la paloma de Venus vuela sobre la Esfinge*. In the lines on the death of Rafael Núñez, when the black bark of Charon reaches the other side, Núñez sees the Cross standing, and finds at its foot a frozen corpse: *el helado cadaver de la Esfinge*.

For Rubén Darío there was still poetry in religion: *entre la catedral y las ruinas paganas.* A creed was not merely a business proposition for saving one's own soul, nor yet (as Swinburne said) a rod; Rubén Darío was too gentle, too unselfish, for that. His eroticism was the penalty for his poetic sensitiveness, perpetually titillated by the legend of Leda and the Song of Songs. Yet it was this sensitiveness which made him the poet he was. Rhythm, which at a political meeting could be a trumpet or a cornet, could also be a wave of the sea or the fall of a snowflake:

> es un ritmo de onda de mar,
> o un caer de copa de nieve.

We must remember, too, that though he had known the sea from his earliest youth he would have been already grown up, in Chile, when he first saw a snowflake or an icicle. Again, nothing is more like him than the glimpse of Aubrey Beardsley in Paris, who 'slipping by like some shy sylph, with charcoal, snow and ashes, gave flesh and soul to his fancy'.

> Aubrey Beardsley se desliza
> como un silfo zahareño.
> Con carbón, nieve y ceniza
> da carne y alma al ensueño.

4

If the swan—sense or poetry—is Rubén Darío's chief symbol, more telling in many ways is the butterfly. It may be the *verso sutil que pasa o se posa*; or the butterfly which is invisible:

> Divina Psiquis, dulce mariposa invisible.

But if the nightingale sings to the rose in ancient Greek, the butterfly may settle on a nail of the True Cross; Rubén Darío, as usual, was mixing his mythologies, and steering between the pagan ruins and the cathedral.

The pre-Raphaelite Princess of the *Sonatina* (probably suggested by *A Royal Princess* of Christina Rossetti) would like to be a butterfly just out of the chrysalis. Darío in an earlier poem wished his own soul might be one when he said: *Mi alma quiere dejar su crisálida*, or referred to *La crisálida de mi alma entristecida.* 'Oh', the Princess exclaims, 'that *I* were a butterfly that escaped from the chrysalis!'

> ¡Oh, quién fuera hipsipila que dejó la crisálida!

The word *hipsipila* is not yet in the dictionaries and has puzzled most of the commentators. It must, of course, mean a butterfly, because it is something that comes out of a chrysalis; but in another well-known poem, the introduction to *Cantos de vida y esperanza*, even that help is denied. Gentle Hypsipyle sips the rose:

Hipsipila sutil liba en la rosa,

and the difficulty is increased by the word *liba* (sips), even in the latest edition, being misprinted *iba* (was going).

Hipsipila is not merely a butterfly, but a particular kind of butterfly, which might be mistaken for a dragon-fly by someone who was not an entomologist. It was illustrated by Pieter Cramer, a Dutch painter of butterflies, in 1777; and he, remembering a rather disreputable Greek story, called it *Hypsipyle* from its strong scent. Unfortunately it had already been christened *lybia* in the mistaken belief that it came from Africa; and that name has priority for the scientific name which is now *Eueides lybia*. It, and other species very like it, are found commonly in tropical America, including Nicaragua where Rubén Darío may have watched it as a boy. Dr. G. B. Longstaff, a familiar Oxford figure of fifty years ago and author of a book of reminiscences entitled *Butterfly hunting in many lands*, caught *hipsipilas* and their relations in Trinidad. 'I took a female', he says, 'and noted that it had a slow flight, also a peculiar scent, which was strong and compared at the time to that of acetylene.' After other remarks on the butterfly's habits, he adds that it lays its eggs on a species of passion-flower. The caterpillar has two horns on its head, but the chrysalis is not well-known. The butterfly sips the honey of flowers—not roses, but the showy Christmas Poinsettia. The smell is protective, intended to drive away birds and men and other enemies; it is only produced when the butterfly is attacked. But to attract one another, both sexes produce another scent which is delicate and agreeable. 'Their long, narrow wings give them a look all their own, while their colours—generally beautiful, pure and deep (golden or brown) render them, like the (great blue butterfly) *Morpho*, a real ornament to the Central American landscape.'

There can be no doubt, then, that *hipsipila* is a butterfly; but what a poem Rubén Darío might have made of its entomology! He remembered the great blue butterfly in his late Mexican poem,

Tutecotzimi, 'in its dress of rich velvet, fanning the mud with its double fan':

> e intacta con su veste de terciopelo rico,
> abanicando el lodo con su doble abanico,
> está como extasiada la mariposa azul.

The butterfly is also a symbol of classical antiquity, the image of transformation, of Goethe's *Stirb und werde* (die and be born); and there is also the butterfly of Schubert's music, 'born of earthly sorrow, shot through with the radiance of an eternally melancholy beauty', Alfred Einstein said.

5

Rodó (the great Uruguayan of his time) opined, rather tartly, that whatever else Rubén Darío might be he was not the poet of America. Salinas tended to find him most Latin-American in his effusiveness and worship of Paris. Actually, the few poems of the tropics are among his best. In the mass of occasional verse, improvizations for albums and inscriptions for fans, which fill so many pages of the collected editions, it is the tropical poems more particularly which 'enlarged the circumference of the imagination' with the strange force and obvious truth of their tropical scenery. In England, a poet would watch 'from dawn to gloom' the lake-reflected sun or the yellow bees in the ivy. In Nicaragua ... 'It is mid-day; the whole island is on fire. The rock burns and the sky shoots forth flames'.

> Un mediodía
> toda la isla quema. Arde el escollo:
> y el azul, fuego envía.

By late afternoon, the siesta is over and the hour of sunset approaches; there is a freshness on the seashore, calcined by the sun of the tropics. 'There is a soft breath of sea-breeze, and the west seems a forest lit up by purple flame. Over the sand, great crabs leave the illegible scrawl of their tracks':

> Sobre la arena dejan los cangrejos
> la ilegible escritura de sus huellas.

There are rose-coloured shells with golden reflexions; smaller shells and fragments of starfish form a carpet resounding to the tread of the echoing beach.

These poems, *Mediodía* and *Vesperal*, date from 1907, and were published in the *Poema del Otoño*; but an earlier poem of 1891 is even more startling: the *Sinfonía en gris mayor* printed in *Prosas profanas*. It might seem, from the name, to be mere 'hommage à Gautier'. Actually it is a grey vision of the port of Acajutla in Salvador. The sea is a vast crystal covered with quicksilver, reflecting the smooth plate of a sky of zinc. Far flights of birds stain the polished surface of pale grey. The sun is a round, opaque glass, stumbling towards the zenith with the step of an invalid. The seabreeze is stilled in the shadow, making a pillow of its own piping. The waves, moving their leaden bellies, seem to groan beneath the jetty. And there, sitting on a coil of rope, is an old sailor, smoking his pipe and thinking of the shores of a vague, far, foggy country . . . The tropical siesta comes. The old sea-dog falls asleep. The key of grey enwraps everything:

> Ya todo lo envuelve la gama del gris.

Año nuevo, the poem printed next before the *Sinfonía en gris mayor*, was written three years later; for New Year's Day, 1894. It is not tropical; the scenery is planetary, sidereal. It is one of the most imaginative and fully-realized poems that Rubén Darío ever wrote; yet it is like a box of toys. It was a favourite with Antonio Machado, who at one time would walk along the Canalillo and round the Colina de los Chopos of the old, pre-totalitarian Residencia de Estudiantes, chanting it in his soft voice. *La página blanca*, another of the *Prosas profanas*, was written at Buenos Aires in 1896. It introduces the figure of Death, dreaded but inspiring memorable poetic visions. Death, for Rubén Darío—as for Lorca, Cocteau and even for Calderón—was a woman: *la ignorada emperatriz y reina de la Nada*. Here, she is riding across the desert on a dromedary: the Pale One, the One in dark raiment, the Invincible Queen:

> Y camina sobre un dromedario
> La Pálida,
> la vestida de ropas obscuras,
> la Reina invencible, la bella inviolada,
> La Muerte.

'But no!' cries one of the Centaurs in an earlier poem. 'Death? Yes, I have seen her; not wasted, no, nor withered. No crooked scythe she carries; her face is not afflicted. The semblance of Diana, virgin and pure as she is; in her look is the grace of the bride of to-morrow, and she brings with her a garland of roses from the stars'.

> ¡La Muerte! Yo la he visto. No es demacrada y mustia,
> ni ase corva guadaña, ni tiene faz de angustia;
> Es semejante a Diana, casta y virgen como ella;
> en su rostro hay la gracia de la núbil doncella
> y lleva una guirnalda de rosas siderales.

The sidereal imagery is one of the discoveries of Rubén Darío. We found it in *Año nuevo*; we find it again in *Los tres reyes magos*, a poem on the three Magian kings. 'I know it all', says Baltasar, the third king, 'from the pure morning star that shines in the diadem of Death.'

> Todo le sé por el lucero puro
> que brilla en la diadema de la Muerte.

Vuela la mágica ilusión . . . was it all a magic illusion, the poetry of Rubén Darío, a conjuring trick performed to a tune from an operetta of the 1890's? No; there is something left in the *caja pandórica*, in Pandora's box; some real achievement and hope for the future. It is right at the bottom of the box, just now; completely out of fashion; but one day, a delicate hand will take it out and dust it, and it will fly again. Rubén Darío will come back.

NOTE ON THE TEXT OF THE POEMS

It may seem impertinent for a foreigner to attempt to add anything to the immense learning and research devoted to the text and chronology of the poems by the Mexican scholar, Alfonso Méndez Plancarte. In *Rubén Darío: Poesías completas*, Madrid, 1952, we have at last a critical edition which even a classical scholar can respect. The following additional notes and emendations are suggested with all due deference.

AZUL. *Estival*. The first printing (*La Epoca*, Santiago de Chile, Sept. 25, 1887) and the first edition have *africana*, corrected in later editions to *indiana*, since it is a question of a Bengal tiger. But in line 16 *kanguro* (kangaroo) has to remain because of the rhyme with *obscuro*. Line 106: for 'torrentes' read, with *La Epoca* and first edition, *torrente*. Line 108: originally *un príncipe gallardo*; the *Príncipe de Gales* (The Prince of Wales) was an afterthought.

Anagke. In the first edition the title is given in Greek capitals ΑΝΑΓΚΗ, the gamma made by knocking off one arm of a T. This should be latinized as *ANANGKE*, or (in *Canto a la Argentina*, 277) ANANKE. Méndez Plancarte finds the same spelling in the short story *Rojo*. It is hard, nowadays, to understand the consternation caused by the last eight lines, or what could have led even Valera to suppress them. Blake said much the same: 'Did he smile his work to see? Did he who made the Lamb make thee?'

Sonatina. Add to Méndez Plancarte: line 26, *halcón*: some editions give 'balcón' or 'balón'; *el balón encantado* is a possible emendation. Line 26, *los cisnes unánimes*: Mapes (*L'influence française*, 68) prints, though without comment, *inánimes*, which is more satisfactory.

Trébol II. Line 9: 'A Teócrito y Possin', read Poussin?

CANTOS DE VIDA Y ESPERANZA. *A J. Enrique Rodó*: line 75, for 'iba' read *liba*.

Salutación del optimista. Lines 4 and 5: the metre demands that these lines should be re-set:

> Lenguas de gloria. Un vasto rumor llena los ámbitos;
> mágicas ondas de vida van renaciendo de pronto.

The word *mágicas* is generally printed as forming part of line 4.

Line 43: Díez-Canedo emends *esa epifanía* to *ese pentecostes*, the reference being not to the Three Kings led by the Star of Bethlehem, but to the Holy Ghost and the tongues of fire seen burning on the heads of the Apostles on Whitsunday.

A Roosevelt. Line 47: there is no need to introduce 'por' before 'Dios', giving a hyper-metric syllable. The poet regarded the word *Roosevelt*, correctly, as trisyllabic. Read:

> Se necesitaría, Roosevelt, ser Dios mismo.

Tarde del Trópico. Line 15: The earlier version has *dulce y profunda*, for the later *triste y profunda*. The effect is quite different; the poet must have changed his mind. For the last stanza, all editions of the *Cantos de vida y esperanza* print (lines 21–24):

> Cual si fuese lo invisible . . .
> cual si fuese el rudo son
> que diese al viento un terrible
> león !

The reading of the earlier version:

> Cual si hablase lo invisible . . .
> cual si fuese . . .

should probably be restored. Cf. the repetition of *felino*, in lines 1 and 3 of the poem to Isadora Duncan, *La bailarina de los pies desnudos*, in *El canto errante*. E. Díez-Canedo, *Letras de América*, 94 (Colegio de Mexico, 1944) emends thus

> Iba en un paso rítmico y felino
> a avances dulces, ágiles o rudos,
> con algo de animal y de divino,
> la bailarina de los pies desnudos.

This was accepted by Méndez Plancarte.

Por el influjo de la primavera. Line 29: for 'fémina' read *femmina*. The Italian quotation is from the libretto of Mozart's *Don Giovanni*.

EL CANTO ERRANTE. *Salutación al águila*. Line 3: there is some doubt whether to read *anillados* or *anillos*. The metre favours the former; the 'anillas' of some editors is not possible. A war-time edition in Spain suppressed this poem for being, presumably, too favourable to the United States.

En elogio del Ilmo. Sr Obispo . . . Line 29: the poet evidently meant *manuales*, not 'pedales'.

NOTE ON PROSODY

Perhaps the best description of Rubén Darío's hexameters is that given by Pedro Henríquez Ureña, *La versificación española irregular*, 2 ed. Madrid, 1933: p. 323, 'free verses, without rhyme, in a long fluctuating series vaguely suggesting the sound of the hexameter'. Some are 'accentual' in that they follow the beat or 'ictus' of the metre; others are more in the spirit of Carducci's *poesie barbare*—'barbarous' because they do not necessarily keep to the metrical ictus of the Latin but follow the rhythm produced by the speech-accent of the modern words. Some again fall into pairs with a certain air of Latin elegiac couplets.

In the following examples the acute accents represent the rhythm, the vertical lines the metre. To avoid complication the secondary accent is not shown.

> | Yó te sa | lúdo a | hóra | cómo en | vérsos la | tínos

would be a tolerable accentual hexameter (if it had a caesura); the speech-accents of the words coincide with the ictus of the metre. But

> | te sálu | dára an tá | ño || Públio O | vídio Na | són.

is a 'barbarous', Carduccian pentameter because the speech-accents conflict with the metrical ictus. It might be compared with Ovid's

> | qui tríbus | ánte quá | ter || ménsibus | órtus é | rat;

and a similar type of Latin pentameter, from the *Epicedion Drusi*, was actually quoted by Rubén Darío—one which both he and Carducci would have read:

> quae fúit ánte méum tan génerósa tórum.

This, like the line of Propertius mentioned in the text, shows the speech-accent not merely in conflict with the metrical ictus, but going right across it.

This conflict between rhythm and metre is found in Spanish poetry as well as in Latin; the flow of a Spanish verse is a combination of two accents, a resultant of two forces: speech-accent and metrical ictus. In the first eclogue of Garcilaso, the basic form of the verse, where rhythm and metre coincide, is found in the first two lines. To avoid complication the secondary accent is not shown.

> El | dúlce | lamen | tár de | dos pas | tóres
> Sa | lício | junta | ménte y | Nemo | róso.

In the third and fourth lines there are variations.

> Hé | de can | tár, sus | quéxas | imi | tándo
> cú | yas o | véjas | al can | tár sa | bróso . . .

These lines depend, for their musical effect, on the fact that the reader or listener has already the basic rhythm in his head and notes the variation with pleasure. Line 5 is once more in the basic rhythm of the metre:

> e | stában | muy a | téntas, | los a | móres

but the sixth has a new variation:

> De | pacér | olvi | dádas, | escu | chándo,

The variations prevent the flow of the lines from becoming monotonous.

This, of course, is art-poetry, carefully composed on an Italian pattern; but the same principles may be observed in the Spanish ballads. In the short *Romance del Conde Arnaldos* there are six different ways in which the speech-accent can differ from the metre. The basic accentuation is:

> | Quién hu | biése | tál ven | túra; ·

but in the second line the accent is widely different from the metre:

> | Sóbre | las á | guas de | már.

The third and fourth lines follow the metre, but the fifth and sixth differ.

> | Con ún | falcón | en la | máno
> | la cá | za í | ba ca | zár.

So do the seventh and eighth:

> | vió ve | nír ú | na ga | léra
> | que a tié | rra quié | re lle | gár.

Other variations are:

> | arrí | ba los | háce an | dár . . .
> | Allí | fabló el | cónde Ar | náldos.

Lope could convert the 8-syllable *versos de romance* into the two halves of an accentual hexameter:

> ¿Cómo permítes, cruél
> después de tantos favóres . . . ?

This he did by combining a verse of the type

> sobre las aguas de mar

with

> con un falcón en la mano.

It is, after all, a well-known principle of Latin hexameter verse that the speech-accent and the metrical ictus—the rhythm and the metre—need not coincide in the first half of the line, though they do so towards the end. That, too, is the principle of the English hexameters of Robert Bridges; but it seems, consciously or unconsciously, to have been a principle of Spanish verse of many kinds, in all ages.

The line from *In memoriam Bartolomé Mitre*:

> Recordando el hexámetro que vibraba en la lira de Horacio

is not a hexameter which Horace would ever have allowed to 'vibrate on his lyre'. It suggests, rather, a 7-foot line like

> | Vitae | summa bre | vis spem | nos vetat | inco | are | longam,

though Rubén Darío cannot resist dactyls in the second half, instead of trochees. The last line of this poem, invoking Virgil, might be explained in the same way:

> y a Virgilio latino, guía excelso y amado del Dante.

E

IV

ALFONSO REYES

I

ALFONSO REYES must be the most Latin of all Latin-Americans; but unlike other leaders of Latin-American civilization he has his roots firmly planted in Greek. He has not been the first to do that. Bolívar, the Liberator, was seldom without his French versions of Homer and Plutarch. Rubén Darío had a vision of Greece through the windows of Versailles; Enrique Rodó was led to a more genuine Greece by Leconte de Lisle; Lugones apparently translated Homer himself. Alfonso Reyes, at the age of twenty when he was supposed to be reading law, sat up in an attic looking over the roofs of Mexico City to learn Greek and read it. 'In 1908', he says, 'I was reading the Greek plays on Electra . . . Those words came from far away yet were close to me, seemed part of my surroundings; and the books, witnesses of so much affection and despair, became confidants and counsellors...' Literature (he explains) did what it was meant to do in providing a cure or treatment, without which he might have been wrecked in the whirlpools of adolescence. 'I do not know whether this is the true meaning of humanism; my *Religio grammatici* may seem too sentimental; but once we have found a standard we have a right to use it in any way we can.'[1]

Now that he had justified his passion for Greek as something that mattered in life, it was as if he had created a miniature Greece for his own use: one that was permanently his. He could venture among Greek things naturally, with no fear of romantic archaism, or of what he called 'lyrical compromises' between those days and ours. A late example of this life-long passion is the admirable translation of the *Iliad* which began to appear in 1951, and the delightful commentary in Sonnets, *Homero en Cuernavaca*, written as it were, in the margins.

The 'Latin' of his Latin-Americanism must be taken literally too. Ever since the Spanish arrived on the American continent there have been people among them who read the Latin language with pleasure and wrote it with elegance, particularly in Mexico and Colombia.

The best Mexican poet of the eighteenth century, Rafael Landívar (born in Guatemala), wrote entirely in Latin; and for that reason his long poem in classical hexameters, *Rusticatio Mexicana*, is more alive to-day than it would have been in neo-classic Spanish *octavas*. The expulsion of the Jesuits by the government of Charles III hindered the development of Latin studies in Mexico; yet **Padre** Hidalgo, the paladin of Mexican independence, might have been a character out of Virgil, and a copy of the Valencia edition of Virgil (1777) with Spanish translations facing the Latin, found not long ago in Mexico City, may actually have belonged to Padre Hidalgo himself, for three of the five volumes bear his name or the name of someone else called Hidalgo. This edition contains prose translations of the *Eclogues*, *Georgics* and the first six books of the *Æneid* attributed to Luis de León—a fact which seems to have escaped most commentators except Ochoa. His verse translations are known, but his authorship of the translations in prose has been dogmatically denied.

'I cannot mention Padre Hidalgo', Reyes said at the Mexican commemoration of Virgil's two-thousandth birthday, 'without stopping to express the charm I find in this truly Virgilian figure. He was well read, and had caught a breath of that Jacobin spirit which was blowing through the world from France. His enemies called him *afrancesado* "Frenchified", which in those days was equivalent, more or less, to what now would be called a "red": a man of new and subversive sensibilities. He was well aware of the commotion going on in Europe; but, from close by, he seemed an affable parish priest, not too severe with his neighbours or too exacting with the moral lapses of human nature—a good Christian, in short.'

Padre Hidalgo was a sociable man, a village philosopher, a great talker; but he was also studious, full of intellectual curiosity and enterprise, and not averse from manual labour. The absurdities of the economic and legal systems of the colony prevented him from growing what he wanted to grow. In vain he tried to plant vines, breed silk-worms; the government rooted up his vineyards and cut down his mulberry trees, and it may have been opposition from Spanish officials which first opened his eyes to the meaning of the movement which was pointing towards independence. 'So', Alfonso Reyes said, 'we can imagine him equally well with a plough or a sword, like the heroes in Virgil. His gentleness should not deceive us. An inner fire consumed him, and soon set the whole country in a blaze. . . . That is how he appears to us in that golden

episode of our Mexican Æneid, calling his parishioners at midnight
with sticks and *machetes* by ringing his church bell, and bringing
on the social revolution that was to lead to his own death. This
Virgilian union of agriculture and poetry was the dream of Padre
Hidalgo; but (Reyes adds) we have not realized it even yet.'
'Latinity', he says again, 'is not only a historical force but an
evolutionary one.' 'Already in my time we students no longer
learnt Latin. In the seminaries—which we in Mexico call the
colleges kept by priests—one had to accept their barbarous *latinajos*;
but most of us passed from one lay school to another without ever
meeting with Latin of any kind, which seemed to us *antigualla
de iglesia*' (old junk of the Church). 'Personally', he continues, 'I
should like to see Latin provided for those on the left wing; for I
do not see the advantage of giving up conquests already achieved,
and I should like the humanities to become the natural vehicle for
everything that is autochthonous in Mexico.'[2]

2

  Latin achieved Mexican independence through social revolution.
Sometimes, however, it was merely repetitive. The storm which
broke on Padre Hidalgo was to break again a hundred years afterwards on the contemporaries and friends of Alfonso Reyes; and
Mexico entered once more on a period of civil war with all its
horror and degradation. Nowadays a European can understand
what that meant in terms of war, but only a Mexican can realize
the full horror of it. Most foreign critics have too little historical
imagination or too little sympathy with the country, or they have
been misled by sectarian propaganda. No criticism of Mexico is
justifiable from citizens of other nations unless they realize that for
twenty years, at the beginning of this present century, the country
was in a state of war, inter-war, and post-war: 'wars worse than
civil', BELLA PLUS QUAM CIVILIA. Of course there were 'lawless
roads'; of course there was 'robbery under law'. We do not need
best-sellers by popular authors to tell us that. 'They took my
garden', an old lady said to me; 'but I can still grow plants in pots.'
That is typical of Mexican stoicism, worthy of the choruses of Greek
tragedy, which Reyes noted 'preach submission to the gods;
that is the great, clear lesson in ethics to be derived from the ancient
Greek theatre'.
  Few Mexicans were able to profit by it, however; and by 1917

the poet Enrique González Martínez stood almost alone in maintaining some steadiness in intellectual outlook. For the writers, too, were involved in the war. If not in the actual fighting (though they often were) they served in official agencies and government offices—the most deadening form of war-work for an imaginative writer. We in Britain, at any rate, have found it so; the permanent civil servant may write well, even admirably, but the 'temporary' rarely outgrows the style and mental arrogance which he mistakenly acquired in 'the office'. The return of the Mexican painters from Paris in 1914 led to the great Mexican school of murals; but the writers became involved in war subjects, and it is still too soon to estimate the real place of talented novelists like the authors of *Los de abajo*, *El águila y la serpiente*, or *Se llevaron el cañón para Bachimba*. González Martínez kept his head, and his classical serenity—at a price; and later it was he who, remembering Verlaine and what he had said about rhetoric, called upon all poets speaking Spanish to wring the neck of the swan—*Tuércele el cuello al cisne*—the symbolical swan of Baudelaire, Verlaine and Rubén Darío. During the war in Mexico, however, his poetry became a longing for the blue, distant pride of the high mountains:

> Y quise la soberbia azul de la montaña

—a pride that would never listen, or loftiness let in a thought of prayer, while the despairing plaints of men anxiously furrowed the empty earth's wide spaces:

> soberbia que no escucha, orgullo qui no deja
> llegarse a la plegaria, mientras la humana queja
> ansiosamente surca los ámbitos vacíos.

Or he could console himself with the memory of how on the high hills, an acrid scent of pollen infected the light rustle of the nocturnal breezes:

> un acre olor de polen contaminó los vuelos
> de las nocturnas auras.

López Velarde, a contemporary of Alfonso Reyes, had found poetry in a Mexican country town at peace, and then again in a village when war had passed over it and shattered it.

LA BIZARRA CAPITAL DE MI ESTADO

> Now I will sing in all sincerity
> the strange, remote chief town
> of my own small state, where
> skies are cruel and all the earth is coloured red.

Universal frigidity
always about it, and the lowered eyelids
of modest maidens with apple-cheeked complexions
just as you see on the covers
wrapping boxes of raisins.
Papists Peter the Hermit would have approved of,
and Jacobins from geological ages,
who'll always be hating one another
in all good faith.
A mountain that is typical,
looking exactly like a bucking bronco,
and on its back a chapel, put there
to venerate the Holy Virgin.
                                                    Steep hills
and sudden sharp descents, which are always
rather a bad joke.
There's a cathedral too, and one big bell—
bigger still when you hear it ringing the first thing
in the morning, the crow of the first cock,
and again at Ave Maria; it makes me sorry
the Pope's not there to hear it.
For then, religion calls persistently,
just as if the one complaint most urgent
were those metallic sound-waves;
and hearing at once the concentrated clamour
in bronze notes that call from soul to soul again,
we feel that all the waters
of baptism were running in our very bones,
and once again have made clean our hearts within us.

EL RETORNO MALÉFICO

Best not go back at all, or near the village:
an Eden upside down, and not a sound heard
in all the mutilation of bombardment.

The ash-trees stand there crippled,
like village elders about the big domed church,
only repeating the protests of the tower
shot through and through in gusts of revolution.

Then there was rifle-fire, scoring the surface
of every whitewashed wall
in the spectral village street;
meaningless black-lined maps,
waiting there to be seen by a prodigal son
on his doorstep once again
just as it's getting dark: the unlucky moment
when the light of a one-wick lamp has told him
his hope has ended in nothing.

The clumsy key that had gone all rusty
turned in the lock at last, grinding and grating.
There, in the long-shut passage
that led within, two respectable
old medallions in plaster
frowning still through their sporific eyebrows.
They look across, say to each other 'what's *he* want?'

Then I'd go in still further, tread like a stranger:
come to the fateful courtyard
where the well would be, lost in reflection;
with the old leather bucket,
ever dripping its categorical drip
like an old song's burden: dripping, weeping . . .

But the sun's inexorable: gay and reviving,
making the fountains warm—baptismal fountains
where once my own long dream would plunge.
Ants are at work again.
Out on the roof you hear that birds are busy.
Here and there in the cobwebs, something buzzing.
My love for it all is like an iron ring,
fixed in the stone above a funeral vault . . .
The church tower's new, with an unaccustomed bell-note;
rejuvenated altars.
Amorous pairs walk out;
girls get engaged, humbly and naturally,
giving their hands through the half-open doors
by the light of theatrical street-lamps;
A girl up there, singing away,
some old, old song to a piano;
The gendarme with his whistle . . .
. . . My grief is personal, reactionary.

3

That is López Velarde. Alfonso Reyes was in Europe when the
Mexican civil war began. His father, General Bernardo Reyes,
was a distinguished soldier who, when governor of one of the
northern states (Nuevo León), had proved an efficient and enlight-
ened administrator, and had even introduced a workmen's com-
pensation act before Lloyd George. There was a powerful *Reyista*
party, and at one time Bernardo Reyes was considered the most
likely successor to Porfirio Díaz in the presidency. He was killed
early in the war. His son, Alfonso, always remembered the
rambling sunny house at Monterrey; there is something of 'orient

and immortal wheat' in it, and the poem falls on English ears with
an unconscious echo of the seventeenth century Thomas Traherne.

> Todo el cielo era de añil;
> toda la casa, de oro ...
> Cada ventana era sol.
> Los corredores tendían
> arcos de luz por la casa.
> En los árboles ardían
> las ascuas de la naranjas,
> y la huerta en lumbre viva
> se doraba.
> Los pavos reales eran
> parientes del sol. La garza
> empezaba a llamear
> a cado paso que daba.

> All the sky was deep blue;
> all the house was pure gold ...
> All of the windows were suns;
> The very passages supported
> arches of light through the whole house.
> On the trees outside, there blazed
> red-hot coals of oranges,
> and the garden's vivid light
> gleamed all golden.
> The imperial peacocks seemed
> of the race of the sun. Flamingos
> were bursting into flames of fire
> at every step they were taking.[3]

There was no point in returning home immediately; soon there
was no home to return to. 'In the last flood', he wrote, 'the river
carried away half our garden and the stables at the bottom of it.
Then the house fell down, and the family were scattered. After
that came the revolution. . . . I went abroad with my fortune on
my back and a star (my own) in my waistcoat pocket. Then one
day I heard that they had cut off my livelihood; and then the four
years' war broke out in Europe.'

For the next ten years Alfonso Reyes lived the life of a wandering
scholar in France and Spain. His first book of verse, *Huellas* (written
between 1906 and 1919, and published in 1922), includes poems
dated from Mexico and others from Madrid. The first are more
'impersonal'; essays in initiation, the Spanish critic, Díez-Canedo,
called them, written, like those of his predecessors, under the shadow
of Rubén Darío and the Mexican poet of the generation before,

Manuel José Othón. Where Mexico appears most clearly is in the
poems which reflect the Spanish seventeenth century. They are
Spanish in their general appearance; but, like many buildings in
Mexico, the Spanish lines are altered and softened, above all in
the ornamentation. They are less severe, less grave; a soft profusion
of decoration adds to the lyrical quality and changes the pitch.
The Madrid verses, on the contrary, hardly allude to Spanish things
or Spanish landscape; they are *modos del ánimo*: states of the spiritual
self, the soul as against the mind or intellect.

He saw through the superficial romanticism of the foreigners'
Spain more quickly than most travellers, and wrote a satirically
romantic poem about it.

> —Quéjome, España, de tí.
> —¿De mí, Coridón, por qué?
> —Tiempo ha que desembarqué
> y nunca he cobrado aquí
> lo que en mis playas dejé.
>
> —¡Ay, Coridón, Coridón,
> que en el lejano Catay
> buscas lo que sólo hay
> adentro del corazón!
>
> —Y porque alejas de mí
> a la dama que soñé:
> que ni sus muros salté,
> ni por sus trenzas subí
> hasta el balcón de su fe.
>
> —¡Ay, Coridón, Coridón!
> Tardado has trescientos años:
> con la dama no hay engaños,
> ¡y habrá cerrado el balcón!
>
> —Quéjome, España, de tí.
> —¿De mí, Coridón, por qué?
> —Con tus amores pequé,
> con tu Dios me arrepentí,
> y con todos me engañé.
>
> —¡Ay, Coridón, Coridón!
> No sabes lo que tu dices:
> reincidencias y deslices
> las flores del alma son . . . [4]

'Spain, I've a grouse against you.' 'Against *me*, Corydon, what for?' 'It's
some time, now, since I came, and yet I can never reclaim things left on the farther
shore.' 'Oh, Corydon, Corydon! You've come as far as Cathay, after things
you'll only find that your own heart put away.'
'Then, I've not found her here, the lady of my long dream; nor sung at the

foot of her stair, nor climbed by the rope of her hair to the balcony of her fame. 'Oh, Corydon, Corydon! You've come three hundred years too late. Women aren't deceived that way, and now the balcony's shut.'

'Spain, I've another complaint.' 'Of *me*, Corydon, what for?' 'Your love was a mortal sin, and your God a penancing; and I've been deceived before.' 'Oh, Corydon, Corydon! You don't know what you've been told; for relapses and wrong turnings are the flowers of the soul' . . .

The poem, frivolous though it may seem in translation, has a double descent from Góngora and Virgil:

A CORYDON, CORYDON, QUAE TE DEMENTIA CEPIT!

Alfonso Reyes became associated with the poets and scholars who rediscovered the poetry of Góngora. He lived at the famous Residencia de Estudiantes at Madrid, and worked with the group of researchers who formed the Centro de Estudios Históricos. He contributed to the *Revista de Filologia Española* under Menéndez Pidal, a review which, in those days, had a standard second to no review of its kind anywhere. The texts of the Spanish classics were generally in a deplorable state; he prepared several valuable new editions, and was among the first to realize the nature of the textual problems with which the editor of Góngora is confronted. By a pocket edition of the medieval Archpriest of Hita—unjustly abused by a foreign critic for its modernized spelling (for in this instance a good critical text is available)—he made the poem approachable to many who would never have touched it. A pirated edition appeared in Chile; and in Spain the little square pocket edition was a particular favourite, for its large-scale map of the Archpriest's wanderings in the Sierra Guadarrama when he met with the grotesque but amorous *serranas*: dairymaids living alone for months at a time in the mountains, like the saeter-girls encountered by Peer Gynt. It was familiar to hardy pedestrians like Enrique de Mesa, the poet, and José Castillejo, the director of all the unofficial education (which meant the modern and efficient education) which there was in Spain at the time. Alfonso Reyes also published an edition of the Poem of the Cid, with a translation into modern Spanish printed opposite the text of Menéndez Pidal; for an introduction to the old poem it is invaluable.

4

By 1924 Mexican affairs had steadied, and Alfonso Reyes was put in charge of the Legation in Paris. The appointment was justified; a succession of important diplomatic posts followed, ending with the embassy in Rio de Janeiro. He was a good diplomat, and took his profession seriously at a time when elder statesmen in Europe were behaving with unbelievable folly; but he never gave up writing, and produced admirable occasional prose, a valuable body of criticism, and poetry which has never had justice done to it. We should not be misled by its apparent light-heartedness. The urbanity concealed a deeply sensitive nature, and a feeling for his fellow men, revealed more often by chance remarks in conversation than in the prose and verse which he allowed to be printed. He did not like his mind to appear in public in shirt-sleeves. He had an elegance of thought unusual in his period. The callousness of some inter-war writers did not touch him; everything he wrote shows a finely sensitive mind trained to respond sympathetically to all the intellectual currents of his time.

Different countries have affected his poetry in different ways. He responded to Spain in the light-hearted, anti-romantic manner of *Las quejas*—the 'complaints' already illustrated—and to the fanciful Toledan legend of *El mal confitero* (The Wicked Confectioner).

EL MAL CONFITERO

Now Toledo's a town of ecclesiastics.
For one night only in the year
domestic grapes
provide a pale light wine;

one whose flavour produces the afterglow
of its namesake marzipan,
predisposing the mind meekly and duly
to receive unto itself the sweet savour
canonical
of the fine black grapes preserved in brandy.

The church, we know too well,
will tolerate gluttony;
for every desire a dispensation,
for every bonbon a special bull.

The finest caster sugar pours
down the cathedral transparency;
while in her arms the Virgin rocks
a sweet little god, an eatable god,
all salmon-pink and rose;
and oh! the rich slices I'd cut from the Alcázar,
were it not granite but almond paste!

The church, we're aware, will tolerate gluttony!
and I know a nun who is sugar sweet.

The heaven's enamoured of her hair,
like threads of holden honey;
she'll make an electuary out of nuts
and even one from contemptible carrots,
spiced cider, and crystallized peel, sugared rose-leaf,
the carroway essence of Alexandria,
and so many other things that there's never an end.

But what of that strange confectioner
who of sugar and almonds and grated nutmeg
made articles of belief?
The Pentecost and the Trinity,
Ascension and Corpus Christi too,
and a Jesus almost too good to be true
with an almond just where his heart would be.

But there are rules to every art,
and every figure has his part.
And so he made a Lucifer
whose face was strong, bitter and long;
and instead of a heart, he gave him
an almond of surpassing bitterness.

What a shock for the *madres*! Could death itself be lurking
even among harmless sweets?
In a season so tranquil
could there be verdigris on the pots and pans?

Well I know there are rules to every art,
and every figure must bear his part.

But soaking bitter almonds in syrup,
even those that have gone to form the heart!
Such charity may be excused
In my opinion.

Dissemble a Lucifer so subtly
that he be confounded with Christ himself?
Such charity may be excused
in my opinion.

Oh, artist true!
That's better for you:
you'll not sell me your bitters in syrup,
if I'm to know bitterness
in my own heart.[5]

The best of his early memories of Mexico are found in the poem
Infancia: trappers, rough-riders, cowmen, rural gendarmerie, ballad-
singers, brewers, foundry-workers, miners—most of the real Mexico,
in fact.

INFANCIA

Once I lived with the hunters and trappers,
who'd keep the barrel of a rifle
stored away in a tube of oil,
after they'd first knocked off with a hammer
the foresight and backsight.
'You see', they said to me, 'those things only stop you
taking a real effective aim'.

Then I went to live with the roughriders;
never mounted but bareback, or at most
they'd ride with a halter or a bit,
guiding only with the voice, and hardly
giving the lightest lift to the body
or pressure in from the knee.
'You see', they said to me, 'things like stirrups
are only stuff for city bastards'.

Then I went to live with the cowmen
who smelt of their beasts.
Their hands were chapped; the skin was cracking,
because nothing can harden so much
as the heat of a cow's udder,
and the cream that's dry on the skin.

Then I went to live with the rural gendarmerie,
all of them smugglers in their time,
who would play the guitar and play their card-games,
—play with a pistol or a *machete*—
so tough that they never took cover,
even when given something to weep for.

Then I went to live with the ballad-singers
who'd wet their whistle with *mezcál*,
and sing you some of the finest ballads
worthy of Macario Romero,
worthy of Herácleo Bernal;
tales of the battle of Río Bravo,
and of the things that Crispin did—
the one that made a compact with the devil.

Then for a time I lived by the sugar-mills;
watched how the mighty millstone bruised and crushed
the canes, and threw the mash on to one side,
molasses dripping on the other,
which would be concentrated in big boilers—
always thicker and thicker, blacker and blacker.
And then the fields, when dew was rising,
were sweet with the scent of wild rose, moistened in the stream,
but the plantations were always reeking
of cigarettes that were made of maize-leaf.

Then for a time I lived among the brewers,
watching the blending of the hops,
watching the light brown trickling threads;
and then we would go into the ice-cold chamber
where there was always a smell of the sea and of fish,
and where I always wondered why my eyelids
had lost, as it seemed, their natural weight,
and my eyeballs grown much larger.

Then for a time I lived among men of the forges
and knew how to work the bellows;
and when they showed me a furnace
I would put on a pair of darkened glasses.
There were great rushing streams of molten metal;
and there were flames along the floor,
and cranes perched high up in mid air,
and mountains of bright live coals
that coloured half the sky with red.

And then I went to the mines,
watching the windlass turn and coil,
hearing the dynamite charge explode,
going up and down in baskets and lifts,
and talking with the three estates
—the three great ages of the miner—
tigers and peons and barreteros.

Since then I have seen the world, with many lands and peoples;
found great wrongs done while other wrongs were righted.
But, ah me! Every time that I protested,
imagination remembered and called together
hunters and trappers and roughriders and cowboys,
preventive men who were smugglers,
musicians of the market,
men of the sugar-mills and of the mines,
men of the breweries and of the iron-founderies.

And thus I am, in every land, with every people,
commanding in imagination
—while the great day is dawning—
thousands of pitched battles, leading my shadowy levies
of the Sierra Madre del Norte.[6]

Another poem of childish memories came from the reflexion
of the sun in a bucket of water.

LA VIEJA LIRA

i

They are all part of a child's mythology:
scarecrows up in the air,
dark shrubberies in the blacked-out garden,
nodding crests of the tree-tops,
the curtains of the moonlight,
crackling noises in cupboards,
rooms walled-off with plaster and stone; and some things
quite untouchable, dangerous, and holy—
Not all were frightening, not all had been forbidden.

That charming lesser god, the musical cricket,
entoned his minstrel lay; while the cicada
bawled a ballad outside.
Here were mice that were sociable
off to visit their friends above the ceiling;
tables and chairs you could trust—all good companions,
the kind you could talk to yourself with—
and one that was rightly called a 'confidente',
which was a snug settee with bosomy cushions.

ii

A child went all alone,
exploring the temple that Nature had provided,
where (the poets tell us)
all things are living and communicating:
trees that can sing and birds that talk together,
and a fountain of coloured water spouting sky-high.

A bucket left in the sun shot out reflexions
a great cobweb of light, all shimmering.
You dipped your hand in it with joy, and stirred it,
and saw a spectre dancing on the wall.
That was the 'vieja-lira',
a name that's given it by quite humble people,
about the house and the kitchen.

To set the vieja-lira dancing: that was
a game we loved to play
all through the hours called dead—yet living!—
just when children are children,
and not mixed up with people older than they are;
those who go spoiling all the poetry,
the wet blankets and grumblers.

The vieja-lira vanishes completely,
just like a flash of lightning;
a swing that every time gets slower, and ending
by being quite still. It was the soul of the water;
and now the spirit's gone!

Cruel, oh cruel the hand
to spoil such beauty every time it's born!
Pit-a-pat, pit-a-pat, goes the heart; and then
regains once more its restfulness.
      Patient flashing reflexions, vieja-lira,
that come and go. You'll always stay with us,
deep down in the last ditch of our heart of hearts.[7]

A return to Mexico in 1924 produced surrealist visions like *Golfo de Mexico* translated in 'New Directions' by Mr. Dudley Fitts. *Viento en el mar* (Sea breeze), *Caravana* and *Yerbas del Tarahumara* (Herbs of the Tarahumara Indians) belong to the same time and much the same style.

VIENTO EN EL MAR

When we were sailing along the Bahama Channel
the ship was colonized by insects and strange birds.

A bang on the table made the glasses rattle;
and then a disdainful voice,
forgetting Florida, out there in the offing:

'That's just a faint foretaste! That's not America!
You've never been in Rio?
Even the ferns are trees there,
just as they were in the world in its infancy.

If you don't look out, a carnation blooms in your buttonhole,
or else you find your hat spontaneously
flowering with feathers of flamingo colours.

A broom left lying about
begins to have roots growing out of the handle,
and flowers on the tips of all the bristles' . . .

When we were sailing along the Bahama Channel
a voice of thunder boomed in the circle of empty glasses:

'Not know the South at all, you pale-faced strangers?
Humanity still half baked, all this time.
Down there, life can pass over into death,
and death perform the functions that our life does.
A glass of pure water can turn to deadly poison,
a vacuum pump engender butterflies.
Even an idea sometimes becomes General.' . . .[8]

CARAVANA

To-day at last we had news of our lost poet.
There was a murmur of mouth-organs all around him,
and his arms were hanging from the paling stars,
when he stopped his horse for us.

The whole of the women's encampment were clapping hands,
for they were kneading the maize for their tortillas,
All the girls were biting the stems of flowers,
and their elders were sealing tearful bonds of eternal friendship,
along with libations to the deepening daylight.

They carried buckets of water up and down,
and the chief himself got ready
to wash his head and his beard and his hairy chest.

The lusty potters with their seven wives
had already begun to caress the wet, round jars.
The local inhabitants who do nothing, ever,
were lighting immense cigars as long as walking-sticks;
and, for the morning sacrifice,
unblemished lambs for all,
were turning slowly impaled upon the spits,
over the reddening flames of sweet scented logs.

To-day at last we had news of our lost poet,
because he had fallen asleep while still on his horse.
He told us they carried God on the points of their lances,
and that night spread out its acid roses
over the carpets of the morning and evening twilight.[9]

The finest poem Reyes ever wrote is the vision of the Tara-humara Indians.

YERBAS DEL TARAHUMARA

Han bajado los indios tarahumaras,
que es señal de mal año
y de cosecha pobre en la montaña.

F

Desnudos y curtidos,
duros en la lustrosa piel manchada,
denegridos de viento y sol, animan
las calles de Chihuahua,
lentos y recelosos,
con todos los resortes del miedo contraídos,
como panteras mansas.

Desnudos y curtidos,
bravos habitadores de la nieve,
— como hablan de tú —
contestan siempre así la pregunta obligada:
—'Y tú ¿no tienes frío en la cara?'

Mal año en la montaña,
cuando el grave deshielo de las cumbres
escurre hasta los pueblos la manada
de animales humanos con el hato a la espalda.

La gente, al verlos, gusta
aquella desazón tan generosa
de otra belleza que la acostumbrada.

Los hicieron católicos
los misioneros de la Nueva España,
— esos corderos de corazón de león.
Y, sin pan y sin vino,
ellos celebran la función cristiana
con su cerveza-chicha y su pinole,
que es un polvo de todos los sabores.

Beben tesgüino de maíz y peyote,
yerba de los portentos,
sinfonía de estética lograda
que convierte los ruidos en colores;
y larga borrachera metafísica
los compensa de andar sobre la tierra,
que es, al fin y a la postre,
la dolencia común de las razas de hombres.
Campeones del Maratón del mundo,
nutridos en la carne ácida del venado,
llegarán los primeros con el triunfo
el día que saltemos la muralla
de los cinco sentidos.

A veces, traen oro de sus ocultas minas,
y todo el día rompen los terrones,
sentados en la calle,
entre la envidia culta de los blancos.

Hoy sólo traen yerbas en el hato,
las yerbas de salud que cambian por centavos:
yerbaniz, limoncillo, simonillo,
que alivian las difíciles entrañas,
junto con la orejuela de ratón
para el mal que la gente llama 'bilis';
la yerba del venado, el chuchupaste
y la yerba del indio, que restauran la sangre;
el pasto de ocotillo de los golpes contusos,
contrayerba para les fiebres pantanosas,
la yerba de la vibora que cura los resfríos;
collares de semillas de ojo de venado,
tan eficaces para el sortilegio;
y la sangre de grado, que aprieta las encías
y agarre en raíz los dientes flojos.

(Nuestro Francisco Hernández
— el Plinio Mexicano de los Mil y Quinientos —
logró hasta mil doscientas plantas mágicas
de la farmacopea de los indios.
Sin ser un gran botánico,
don Felipe Segundo
supo gastar setenta mil ducados,
para que luego aquel herbario único
se perdiera en la incuria y en el polvo!
Porque el padre Moxó nos asegura
que no fué culpa del incendio
que en el siglo décimo séptimo
aconteció en el Escorial).

Con la paciencia muda de la hormiga,
los indios van juntando sobre el suelo
le yerbecita en haces,
— perfectos en su ciencia natural.

HERBS OF THE TARAHUMARA

Here once more are the Tarahumara Indians.
That's a sign of bad weather,
and of a wretched harvest in the mountains.

Those bare and sun-tanned bodies,
lean and hard in their stained but shining skins,
rough and blackened by wind and sun, enliven
the wide streets of Chihuahua;
slowly, suspiciously,
with all the tight-coiled natural springs of fear contracted,
looking like half-tamed panthers.

Those bare and sun-tanned bodies,
wild inhabitants of the snow-bound regions,
— always calling you 'thou'—
and always answering thus the inevitable question:
'But thou: dost not feel cold, then, on thy bare face?'

A bad year in the mountains,
when it suddenly thaws out, on the high peaks,
and drives down to the towns the roving herds
of human animals with their packs on their shoulders.

The people like to see them,
enjoy the generous, unusual vision
of different beauty to that they are accustomed.

They made them into catholics,
those missionary preachers of New Spain
—gentle as lambs but with hearts as stout as a lion's—
And, with no bread and no wine,
still they celebrate catholic communion
with home-brewed *chicha* ale, and with *pinole*,
which is a powder producing several flavours.

They drink *tesgüino* made of maize and *peyote*—
a most portentous herb, this,
a symphony of most advanced aesthetic,
converting every sound into a colour;
while metaphysical intoxication
repays their wandering in the wilderness,
which is, when all is considered
the common fate of all the races of man.
Champions in the Marathon of the whole world,
and nourished on the bitter flesh of their wild game,
they are the first to be there and be the winners
the day that we leap over the low wall
of our five senses.

Sometimes they bring great nuggets from their well-hidden gold-mines;
and all day long, seated by the roadside,
they pound their lumps to pieces,
watched by the cultured envy of the white man.
To-day they've only herbs inside their knapsacks,
the old time healing herbs they sell you for three ha'pence:
aniseed, lemon-herb and baccharis
alleviating difficult digestion,
along with the severed ear of a dead mouse
for the complaint which people here call 'bilis';
the herb of hunting-spears, the *chuchupaste*,
and the herb of the Indian, that great blood-restorer;

and Jacob's staff that's good for all bumps and bruises,
and antidotes fit for the fevers caught in marshes,
the herb that's called the viper's herb and cures all coughs and colds;
and necklaces made out of the seeds of velvet-beans,
so good against the worst effects of witchcraft;
and the green dragon's blood that tightens up the gums
and holds firm to the root when a tooth is loosening.

Our old Francisco Hernández
—the great Mexican Pliny back in the fifteen-hundreds—
collected over twelve hundred plants with magic powers
from the pharmacopoea of the Indians.
Then came King Philip II;
and he, though not a botanist,
managed to spend some seventy thousand ducats
so that presently that unique herbarium
should be lost through carelessness.
(At least, Padre Moxó would have assured us
that it was not the fault of the great fire
which sometime in the seventeenth century
broke out in the Escurial).

So with the dumb, deliberate patience of ants
the Indians sit collecting in front of them
the little heaps of herbs,
—so perfect in their natural philosophy.[10]

5

The critical opinions of Alfonso Reyes deserve attention. His
more specialized contributions are to be found in the two volumes
on Spanish literature, *Capítulos de literatura española*, in *El Deslinde*;
prolegómenos a la teoría literaria, and in his large and important book
on ancient criticism and rhetoric. But Spanish-speaking America
he explains in this way: 'Arriving late at the banquet of European
civilization, we live by leaping over whole periods; hastening our
step and running from one form to another, without having had
time to mature the one which came before. Sometimes the leap is
daring, and the new form has the look of a dish taken from the oven
before it is properly cooked.'[11] Alfonso Reyes has been claimed, in
the United States as in Cuba, to be exclusively American property:
'Our Alfonso Reyes'. His European side needs emphasis. Mexican
though he is, he is one of the last—though certainly not the least—
of an almost extinct species: 'the good European'.
Tradition weighs less heavily on Spanish-speaking people in

America than it does in Europe; but that tradition is still Latin. The spirit of Mexico depends 'on the tint which the Latin waters have acquired by the time that they have reached us in our home, after flowing for three centuries and washing the red clay of our Mexican soil'. Even thinkers in Britain, he says, 'surveying the scene from the opposite shores of race and language, do not hesitate to recognize that in the upper stories of their own national formation the corner-stones came from Rome. The idea of Latin civilization is wide and elastic; it extends beyond the barriers of seas and continents, religion and language.'

After quoting from his own exquisite Spanish translation of *The Ebb Tide* of Robert Louis Stevenson (*La Resaca*), the episode of the broken-down Englishman reading a tattered school Virgil on a South Sea Island, he adds: 'This is the true image of a moral Robinson Crusoe, starting to rebuild the ruins of his emotional life on some verses of Virgil. . . . The Latin words give the man his place again.'[12]

With good reason, Virgil appears to Mexicans a voice from their own country. From him they learn that nations are founded in sorrow and shipwreck: 'In the adventures of Aeneas going from shrine to shrine to save his household gods, I know many Mexicans who have thought they saw the image of their own misadventures; and I doubt whether we should call him a good Mexican who could read the *Æneid* without being deeply moved by it. The reading of Virgil acts as a ferment on the idea of one's own country, gives it a deeper meaning; with a Virgil in one's hand, one could go down to Hades and return to tell the tale. . . . Do not break the precious instrument. If you do, you will be disarmed while the rest of the world is in process of transformation . . . Latin is a good ship to travel in, and one must look out for storms.'

Virgil is the poet of all peoples. Dr. T. J. Haarhoff has explained what the poet means in the experience of South Africa; and an Australian pupil once remarked: 'How could a people of sheep-farmers not read the *Georgics* at school!' For centuries it was believed that Virgil had foretold the birth of Christ; now it seems that the tale of the Trojans in Italy was like the Spanish conquest of Mexico. The poem of the conquest is, in fact, the *Æneid*, and the adventures of Aeneas might be illustrated by engravings from those books of the sixteenth and seventeenth centuries which relate the travels and adventures of the *conquistadores*: the audiences with *caciques*, the penetration into unknown countries by rowing up the rivers. Indeed

most things that happened to the Spaniards in Mexico seem to
have happened before to the Trojans by the Tyrrhenian Sea. The
events of the *Æneid* are of shorter range than the opening up of
America; but there is a poetic relationship between Aeneas and
Cortés, and between the *caciques* of Latium and the Aztec emperors.

Alfonso Reyes thinks the comparison might be carried further.
In an article published in 1930 he pointed out the likeness between
the attitudes of Montezuma to Cortés and King Latinus to Aeneas.

In the seventh book of the *Æneid*, Aeneas reaches the mouth of the Tiber and
approaches the dominions of the King of Latium, just as Cortés approached those
of Montezuma. Latinus, like Montezuma, was a monarch strongly addicted to
religious practices. Before taking a decision he consulted the augurs and the
oracles. The oracles had foretold to Latinus and to Montezuma, the arrival from a
far country of warlike men who would take possession of the land and dispossess
him of his kingdom. The strangers had been announced to the old king as great
strong men wearing unusual garments. In the same way the couriers of Montezuma announced the arrival of the Spaniards to the Children of the Sun. The
manner in which Latinus received the hundred envoys of Aeneas is the same as
that in which Montezuma received the Spaniards; it was the future rulers who had
arrived, the new masters. Nothing could be done against the divine will,
manifested by the appearance of a comet; it was necessary to submit. 'We knew
you already before you came; we were waiting for you', one king says to the other;
and since the contemplation of holy things has weakened, in both of them, the
springs of action, they think it absurd to oppose the course of destiny and both yield
to a conqueror without fighting.

There remains the nationalist reaction, under Turnus and Cuauhtémoc, the representatives of popular commonsense against official
religiosity; officers who have not been sophisticated by excessive
superstition; but neither Latinus nor Montezuma feel able to save
their peoples. Montezuma, a prisoner by his own wish, is stoned by
his subjects; and Latinus, withdrawn into the depths of his palace,
refuses to make war on the Trojans. Raising his hands to the gods
and the empty air, he pronounces a curse which might have been
directed against Cuauhtémoc, the last defender of the Aztecs: 'Oh
Turnus, for you a terrible punishment is waiting !'

TE, TURNE, NEFAS TE TRISTE MANEBIT
SUPPLICUM

The diverting fancies of a scholar can go even further. The
Mexican emblem—the eagle perched on a cactus with a serpent in
its beak—commemorates the Red Indian tribes wandering in the
wilderness until they found the lake, the mountain, the cactus and
the serpent. There is a curious likeness between the Mexican story

and the simile in the eleventh book of the *Æneid*—taken from the Iliad—describing how Tarchon, the Etruscan, picks Venulus, the Latin, off his horse, carries him off and kills him as he rides.

> So stoops the yellow eagle from on high,
> And bears a speckled serpent through the sky,
> Fastening his crooked talons on the prey:
> The prisoner hisses through the liquid way;
> Resists the royal hawk; and, though oppressed,
> She fights in volumes, and erects her crest;
> Turned to her foe she stiffens every scale;
> And shoots her forky tongue, and whisks her threatening tail.

Æneid XI, 751–6, *Dryden's translation*

This characteristic piece of Mexican heraldry re-appears in one of the later *romances* (ballads) of Alfonso Reyes and in two sonnets. He had been living for some years at Rio de Janeiro, happier and more at home than anywhere else in the world. There are poems in the collection called *Romances y afines* (1945) to prove it. *Ciudad remota* (Far city) reflects the mood of return to the austerity of Mexico City and the severe beauty of the valley of Anáhuac, seven thousand feet above the sea.

> Entre espadas de cristal
> que tajan tu luz radiosa
> ¿de dónde tanto misterio,
> México, ciudad remota?
>
> Vuelo de un águila un día
> que en sus garras desabrocha,
> sobre el peñón de la fábula
> las semillas de tu historia. . . .

Of all the flaming swords of glass that cut your gleaming light in two, whence come so many mysteries, far-off, fantastic Mexico?

The mystery of an eagle's flight, and the talons scattering over all the peaks of fable the seeds of your long fashioning . . .

> ¿Por qué te acercas de lejos,
> México, ciudad famosa,
> y estando cerca de ti
> te me apareces remota?
>
> ¿Que vidrio irreal te aisla,
> te suspende y te arrebola?
> ¿Si del peso de tus nubes
> o de aire tenue te ahogas? . . .

So far, and yet you come near me, Mexico, in all your fame; and yet when
I'm close beside you you seem far away again?
What strange glass cuts you off from me? Hangs you high in afterglow?
Can the thick clouds weigh upon you, or the thin air throttle you? . . .

It was difficult to settle into Mexico after Rio de Janeiro.

> Mercedes, Rio, Mercedes, —
> soledad y compañía,
> de toda angustia remanso,
> de toda tormenta orilla.
>
> Y porque nunca pensé
> y porque yo no sabía
> que hay en el mundo una raya
> donde el mundo es lejanía;
>
> una zona en que las sienes
> se curan de las espinas,
> y el mismo dolor se envuelve
> y a sí proprio se acaricia . . .

How grateful, Rio, how grateful, companionship in loneliness; smooth water
for all my anguish, the farther shore of my suffering.
Grateful, for I'd never a thought, neither have I ever known here in this world
a haven where the world's a lost horizon;
a harbour where the aching brow is healed of the crown of thorns, and sorrow
herself laid by covered with her own caresses. . . .[13]

The sense of mutability, with perhaps a recollection of some lines
in *Le cimetière marin* of Paul Valéry, was in his mind when finishing
the poem *Vaivén de Santa Teresa*:

> ¡Eso que anda por la vida
> y hace como que se aleja!
> ¡Eso de ir y venir, eso
> de huir y quedarse cerca!
>
> ¡Eso de estar junto a mi,
> y hace años que estaba muerta!
> ¡Eso de engañar a todos
> como Zenón con su flecha!
>
> Se enlaza el tiempo en la voz:
> la canción tiene pereza.
> Con ágiles pies, los ángeles
> se dejan venir a tierra.
>
> —Voladores y quieta luna,
> garza de sí misma presa,
> entre arabescos de hojas
> va y no va, rueda y no rueda.

That thing that's there all through our life, yet makes as though to run away; that going and coming back, that strange escaping, and yet standing by!

That seeming to be with me still, and years and years been with the dead! That seeming to deceive all men, like Zeno when the arrow sped!

There's time entangled in a voice, and song that loiters on the path; but angels' feet are agile things if once they deign to come to earth.

—Flying, flying, softly calling, bird with itself held in its bill; in and out the leafy pattern she comes and goes, circles, stays still.[14]

The long history of Mexico has had its bitter moments; the two sonnets, *Cara y cruz del cacto* (observe and reverse of the cactus) bring out two sides of that history.

> En lugar del olivo virgiliano,
> la planta de cuchillo y de ganzúa,
> y el árbol sirve de potencia y grúa
> para izar por el cuello al hortelano.

> ¿Por qué brotan del suelo mexicano
> la cólera, la vibora, la púa,
> la espadaña que en pica se insinúa,
> la garra en guante adentro de la mano?

> Torva mitología nos espera,
> y el crudo mineral nos solicita
> más allá de la miel y de la cera.

> Y la alquimia es adusta de manera
> que la sangre en tezontle precipita
> y sube en amarilla tolvanera.

Here, instead of the olive Virgil knew, are plants all armed with bill-hooks and with knives; and gallows-trees that serve to hoist on high and hang by the neck the gardener where they grew.

Oh, why make Mexico alone the land of wrath to come, the serpent and the spike, the sharp steel point that's fitted to the pike, the claw within the glove upon the hand?

Woe, the mythology awaiting us; and slag, the mineral that leads us on beyond this vale of honey and honeycomb!

Unkind is all our alchemy at home! There's blood congealed in our red building-stone to rise in whirling clouds of yellow dust.

The other view, the other side, is summed up in the second sonnet:

> Así, serpiente reposada, grave,
> hecha cristal de su primer delito,
> sorbido por el cacto de su mito,
> vacunada en su duelo con el ave.

So be it, Old Serpent! Rest on the reward of man's first disobedience, crystal glory; spiked on the cactus of an old, old story, and vaccinated fighting with a bird. [15]

Two late poems, *Silencio* and *Consejo poético* give with delightful urbanity his views on the art of poetry. 'I choose out the word that's thinnest, when I want to curse the thunder. . . . And to all the sound and fury oppose unparagoned silence. . . . Every time, words that are fewer, but every word is a verse now; every poem a heart-beat, every beat a universe. The bounds of the world are shrunken to the size of its deep centre; the instant is made immortal and the fugitive eternal.'[16]

CONSEJO POÉTICO

La cifra propongo; y ya
casi tengo el artificio,
cuando se abre el precipicio
de la palabra vulgar.
Las sirtes del bien y el mal,
la torpe melancolía,
toda la guardarropía
de la vida personal,
aléjalas, si procuras
atrapar las formas puras.

¿La emoción? Pídela al número
que mueve y gobierna al mundo.
Templa el sagrado instrumento
más allá del sentimiento.
Deja al sordo, deja al mudo,
al solícito y al rudo,
nada temas, al contrario,
si en el rayo de una estrella
logras calcinar la huella
de tu sueño solitario.

I think of a number, and—pat!—I've almost found the artifice. Then there yawns a precipice; some vulgarian said just that! The Syrtes of good and ill, melancholy's heavy wings, the wardrobe of discarded things, all that made life personal—away with them, if you would try to trap pure form in poetry.

Emotion? Seek it in numbers that move and govern the world. Tune the sacred instrument to sharper keys than sentiment. Leave the deaf and leave the speechless, the solicitous and redeless; we have naught to fear, we know, if in starlight you shall find but the smallest thought calcined of your long lone dream below.[17]

That is what Alfonso Reyes has done for poets speaking Spanish.

NOTES

[1] Comentario a la *Ifigenia cruel* (1923), reprinted in *Obra poética*, Mexico (1952), p. 295.

[2] Homenaje de Mexico al poeta Virgilio, reprinted in *Tentativas y orientaciones*, Mexico (1944); and, in English, 'Virgil in Mexico' in *The Position of America*. New York (1950), translated by Harriet de Onís.

[3] Sol de Monterrey (1932), *Obra poética*, 121.

[4] Las quejas: sátira de los expatriados (1917), *Ib.* 60.

[5] El mal confitero (1918), *Ib.* 63.

[6] Infancia (1934), *Ib.* 126.

[7] La vieja lira (1940), *Ib.* 170.

[8] Viento en el mar (1924), *Ib.* 89.

[9] Caravana (1924), *Ib.* 90.

[10] Yerbas del Tarahumara (1929), *Ib.* 99.

[11] *Sur*, Buenos Aires (1931), No. 24.

[12] Ciudad remota (1938), *Obra poética*, p. 139.

[13] Envío (1932), *Ib.* 343.

[14] Vaivén de Santa Teresa (1932), *Ib.* 330.

[15] Cara y cruz del cacto (1939), *Ib.* 248.

[16] Silencio (1943), *Ib.* 179.

[17] Consejo poético (1943), *Ib.* 180.

V

JORGE GUILLÉN

I

SPANISH poetry is made with Spanish words. Unamuno was always quoting—and deliberately misquoting—St. John, that the word was there in the beginning; and whatever *logos* once meant in New Testament Greek, the Spanish *palabra*, word (originally *parabola*) is now the stuff with which a poet speaking Spanish has to work, the material which gives his ideas their Spanish form. The initial and final dedications to the collected poems of Jorge Guillén are to those who gave him his language: a parent and a friend; the one taught him the words and the other showed what might be done with them.

Jorge Guillén is of the same generation as Pedro Salinas and of the same Spanish tradition—from Don Francisco Giner to Juan Ramón Jiménez—which inspired the original Residencia de Estudiantes. Guillén taught for a time at Oxford, Salinas at Cambridge. In exile in America, they both became energetic and effective university professors, but have been none the less poets for that. Vision, they always had; Guillén's poetic treatment of reality, Salinas thought, was unique in Spanish.[1] Guillén also had enthusiasm. The various editions of his work have always been called *Cántico*. The word goes back to the poet Berceo about 1220.[2] It was all a canticle, a song of joy, not to the Divinity but to the world and this life. *Fe de vida!* Not that the poet is, or has ever been, an unreflecting optimist. The last poem in his book, though not the latest, seems to have been written on hearing of the death of García Lorca, and is called *Cara a cara*, 'Face to face'. It is a grim prospect.

Many of his poems are 'moments of vision', the enthusiasm of the moment catching sight of a thing for the first time, like Keats first looking into Chapman's Homer. 'Can that poetry be dismissed as intellectual', Salinas asked, 'when it proclaims exactly, for a supreme value in life, the fact of being and nothing more, the simple knowledge of being alive and the almost animal joy of it?'[3] Like Paul Valéry, the poet watches himself emerging from sleep to wakefulness; and, again like Valéry, many of his poems arose from the

sudden presence of rhythms in his head.[4] Guillén tells us so himself.
'I feel a rhythm being unravelled for me from this harsh din':

> Siento que un ritmo se me desenlaza
> De este barullo.

And again: 'The sound gives me a profile, flesh and bone. The
form becomes a saving lifebelt for me':

> El son me da un perfil de carne y hueso.
> La forma se me vuelve salvavidas.
>
> (*Hacia el poema*)

In one of the poems first published in 1950, *Vida extrema*, he writes
of 'Rhythm of breathing, rhythm of the word, so deep the power
that rises in me and sings':

> Ritmo de aliento, ritmo de vocablo,
> Tan hondo es el poder que asciende y canta.

Again, 'And here's a rhythm throbbing. We can hear it'.

> He aquí. Late un ritmo. Se le escucha.

The sound (in spite of what some commentators have said) came
first, 'on the still trembling string, and in the accent, there, at the
cadence'

> En la palpitación, en el acento
> De esa cadencia.

In another late poem, *El concierto* (1950) we read: 'Sound for me,
music, sound, raised to the farther shore; snatch me away within,
where the good fortune lies you made for me when my time should
come; so rising to the music of this great culminating reality, I
participate again in the triumph of the absolute harmony in human
air'.

> Suena, música, suena,
> Exáltame a la orilla,
> Ráptame al interior
> De la ventura que en el día mío
> Levantas.
> Remontando al concierto
> De esta culminación de realidad
> Participio también de tu victoria
> Absoluta armonía en aire humano.

There is, in the original, a balance between sound and sense,
'between the body of the poem and its soul'. Music is supreme
reality.

The rhythms that disentangled themselves for Jorge Guillén were strictly classical, in the Spanish sense. The quotation from San Juan de la Cruz introducing the first book, *Al aire de tu vuelo* (to the air of your winged flight) was not chosen for any mystical meaning it might have but for the metre: the seven-syllable line of which he was so great a master. Juan Ramón Jiménez felt its magic, too, when he named one collection of poems *La soledad sonora* (resounding solitude), and Pedro Salinas in a line from Garcilaso, *La voz a ti debida* (the voice I owe to you); for the line of seven syllables conveys surprise and excitement, while the eight-syllabled ballad-line gives the sense of a narrative pushing onwards. Other collections were called *Las horas situadas*, after a seven-syllabled line by Luis de Léon; or introduced by Góngora, *No son todos ruiseñores* (Not all of them are nightingales), a poem which—like the untranslatable verbal music of Guillén's *Damas altas, calandrias*—a foreigner finds himself saying by heart before he can think what it can mean. This is strictly against the precept of Dr. I. A. Richards, in his *Practical Criticism*; but in Spanish, as with Camoens and Virgil, it is often wise to know a passage by heart, before endeavouring to grasp the 'mere sense'. This group of poems is called by the seven-syllabled verse *El pájaro en la mano* (The bird in the hand): a proverbial saying in Spanish as in English, but also with the feeling of holding in your hand a bird which is trying to fly away. Guillén is a poet whose thoughts fall easily into seven syllables, while most poets speaking Spanish prefer eight.

2

Too much has been made of the 'influence' on Jorge Guillén of Paul Valéry. Guillén did not meet Valéry through the family of his wife, Germaine, the gifted Frenchwoman of unforgettable charm and culture (a good musician, too) whom he married in 1921. He had an introduction to Valéry, and since he talked excellent French he was asked to come again. The influence was on the method of his poetry, rather than on the substance: his preference for classical Spanish verse and strophes. Even when he wrote a poem in lines of varying lengths, every line was a regular Spanish verse. His finish and self-discipline may owe something to Valéry, and to the technique acquired in making a close, parallel translation of *Le cimetière marin* in 1929.[5] He was also asked to make a translation of an essay by Paul Claudel, *A la trace de Dieu*.[6] His prose style benefited, but his own 'positions and propositions' were closer to Valéry than to Claudel, without what he calls *el nihilismo de aquel gran escéptico.* Earlier and lighter prose pieces were printed in *Indice,* 1921 and 1923, where some early poems appeared and have not been reprinted.[7]

Guillén soon eliminated all sentimentalism from his verse. He learnt the lesson of Bécquer: to distinguish ornate, pompous poetry from poetry that was short and bare, which browsed for a moment like a sheep and then bounded away, 'leaving the strings harmoniously vibrating'.[8] All Spanish poetry before the time of Bécquer, classical as well as romantic—though not popular poetry—belonged to the first kind; and the great discovery, the legacy of Bécquer, is this new manner in which the lightest touch of a bird's wing can awake an echo in the depths. The poet, however, counts on the imagination of the reader for the full effect. His poetry belongs almost entirely to this second kind; he hardly ever declaims, but expects the reader to listen attentively and meet him half-way. For this reason, his poetry seems to some readers devoid of feeling. He has reduced the expressive elements to a minimum, especially those which can be catalogued and fitted into a familiar formula.[9]

The fact that Guillén knew Valéry and went to his house has led critics to include him with the Abbé Bremond and the advocates of 'pure poetry'—an association which Guillén himself was the first to disclaim. 'Bremond', he said, 'is a man whose point of view cannot be more opposed to that of any "pure poetry". He represents popular apologetics, the Sunday morning sermon . . . But, how far all this mysticism is, with its ineffable, metaphysical phantoms, from pure poetry as Valéry understands it!'[10]

Pure poetry was all that was left in a poem after taking out everything which was not poetry. 'Pure' was equivalent to 'simple' in the chemical sense of a simple substance; so he preferred to call it simple poetry to avoid the Abbé's double meanings. 'I am firmly on the side of poetry which is carefully composed and complicated, for the poem with poetry and other human things in it too; in fact, a poetry pure enough, *ma non troppo.*'

The idea of pure poetry goes back to about 1885, with Poe, or at least Poe interpreted by Baudelaire: *une poésie dénuée d'éloquence.* Verlaine's *Art poétique* included the drastic *Prends l'éloquence et tords-lui son cou,* which, with González Martínez, became the *Tuércele el cuello al cisne* (wring the neck of the swan) of the well-known Mexican sonnet. Mallarmé went farther. For him, *poésie pure* meant poetry without an object, or without a subject; verbal music, in fact; and Mallarmé often seemed incomprehensible because the value which he gave to words seldom depended on their meaning.[11] In Spanish, verbal music has probably a stronger power of evocation than in French, and increases the impression given by the senses.

The problem of pure poetry was—and indeed still is—one of the problems of our time. How is any kind of poetry possible in an age like ours? Antonio Machado presented the problem by making his Meneses invent a poetry-machine, a *máquina de trobar*, which would be sensitive to the feeling of an unintellectual audience and produce a popular lyric within the comprehension of all. The intellectual lyric, represented first by Juan Ramón Jiménez, and then by Jorge Guillén, was becoming too difficult. If the popular lyric produced by Machado's machine was like commercialized and recorded *Cante flamenco*, the intellectual lyric was the equivalent of contemporary chamber-music. There should be room for various kinds of poetry, as there still is for various kinds of music. Juan Ramón Jiménez is the Debussy of modern Spanish poetry, Jorge Guillén its Ravel or Roussel.

Composition, both in music and poetry, demands a disciplined effort. The situation to-day is not unlike the *Situation de Baudelaire* described by Valéry. All classicism presupposes a romanticism which has gone before it. The essence of classicism is to come after. Order supposes a certain disorder which it comes to put straight. The *pureté* which follows is the result of infinite trial and error in the treatment of language, *opérations infinies sur la langage*; and care for form is nothing but a carefully planned rearrangement of the means of expression. The classical approach, therefore, implies 'voluntary and reflective acts which modify the "natural" production in conformity with a clear and rational conception of man and of art'.[12] But we can only make a work rational, and construct according to plan, by means of a body of conventions including rules of prosody and restrictions on vocabulary. This implies 'rigorous metrics . . . and disciplined effort rather than voluptuousness'. Guillén learnt to overcome the difficulties of the *décima*; but when he adopted the symmetry of regular forms to eliminate his subjective caprices he was only expressing his own personality once more. He also tended to have a vocabulary—a rather restricted vocabulary—of his own.

G

3

Commentators have been inclined to neglect the words which the poet normally uses, but have devoted much time to endeavouring to explain what the poems literally mean; they are paraphrased in Spanish and translated into English, an operation which, at its best, is no more successful than the English versions of Mallarmé by Charles Mauron and Roger Fry. A pioneer attempt was made by Miss Frances Pleak[13] with an introduction by Américo Castro which was afterwards reprinted, and considerably revised, in Spanish.[14] For Casalduero, however, the poetry of Jorge Guillén refuses to be written in prose or even to be paraphrased. What Guillén had to say in verse could not be said in prose. 'His work depends purely and simply on the rhythm; there is no mystic way to meet him.'[15] Later studies have little to add; earlier ones were guarded. The Mexican poet Jaime Torres Bodet, lately President of Unesco, compared the poetry of Jorge Guillén to a drop of rain on a clean pane of glass, concave and convex at the same time, a double refraction through the glass and the water. Salazar Chapela found that Guillén did not see things with his own eyes, but with the eye of the spirit; when one tried to read the book in search of allusions to the world of sense, one would find at every turn a hieroglyphic. (But hieroglyphics can be deciphered by competent scholars, while even a beginner can see which hieroglyphics occur most often.)

Moreno Villa, in his stimulating study on reading the Spanish poets,[16] gives, for Guillén's favourite word, *ser*; 'to be' or 'being'. One might follow the method further, and point to the number of times in which *ser* and *estar* (the two Spanish words for 'to be') are used together or in comparison. It is an elementary fact of Spanish grammar that *ser* is generally associated with what is inherent or permanent, *estar* with what is accidental or temporary; *es libre*, he is a free man; *está libre*, he is free (or disengaged) at the moment. There are exceptions, of course. Death is not usually regarded a temporary state; but the Spanish (more theologically minded, Unamuno would have said, than other peoples) say *está muerto*, he is dead. Unfortunately for the theological view, they also say that of a broken glass or plate, or anything breakable which cannot be mended: *está roto*, it is permanently and not temporarily broken. Conversely, if a man is at all popular, they say *es muy querido*, he is loved permanently through his inherently lovable qualities, though they cannot be sure that he will be loved more than temporarily. With *estar*, in fact, the adjective does not signify a quality which is transitory, but one which has been acquired; the allusion is not to the final state, but to the beginning. *Está gordo* does not mean that, though fat, he will necessarily get thinner, but that lately he has grown distinctly stout, *se ha puesto gordo*.[17]

In Guillén's first poem, *Más allá* (Beyond), there is already an example. 'I exist', he says, 'more, I am here. I breathe.'

> Soy, más, estoy. Respiro.

In the poem *Despertar* (Waking up) he gives other Spanish equivalents of the words *ser* and *estar*. 'I. I now. I here. Awake, being now, being here.'

> Yo. Yo ahora. Yo aquí.
> Despertar, ser, estar.

Earlier in the same poem we read: 'That bulk (i.e. his waking body) feels that it exists now, but is not here':

> Aquel bulto se siente ser, no está.

Paul Valéry said much the same: '*Tu existes . . . Tu es*', *dit l'Amour*; but the remark was written—or at least published—long afterwards, in Canada.[18]

The poem called *Ser*:

> El intruso partió. Puedo ser donde estoy.

is explained (it often happens in Guillén) in the last line, where the opening phrase is varied. *El intruso* is now shown to be grief: *dolor*:

> El intruso dolor — soy ya quien soy — partió.

In *Más verdad* we read: 'To exist in the chain of beings. To be here now.'

> De ser en la cadena de los seres.
> De estar aquí.

The words used most frequently by a poet will tell us a good deal of his state of mind. In the poems of Jorge Guillén, the word *blancura*, for instance, 'whiteness', occurs some twenty times. There is the *blancura* of a sheet, of course, and of a town after a fall of snow. But there is also a *blancura* which is a light rather than a snowfall:

> esta blancura
> Que es una luz aun más que una nevada.

—so much silence converted into pure material substance:

> Tanto silencio convertido en pura
> Materia
>
> *(La noche de más luna)*

and there is the *blancura* of snow preserved, which is an ash-tree:

> ¡Esa blancura de nieve salvada
> Que es fresno!
>
> *(Viento saltado)*

and of 'unmoving cold beneath the firmament':

> De frío inmóvil bajo el firmamento,

which is also:

> Recta blancura refrigeradora.
>
> *(La Blancura)*

Again, there is the stream which is *blancuras en curva* (*El manantial*) and the *blancura* of sheep against a blue sky (*Tarde muy clara*), while a flower, *celinda* (syringa), smells white: *huela a . . . blancura*. Finally there is the *blancura* of the breeze which, on a festive morning, is swollen with celestial blue (*Festividad*).

Words connected with dawn and early morning, *alba*, *albor*, *alborada*, *alboreado*, occur over twenty times in Guillén's *Cántico*. The first two are old words from the poem of the Cid; the third is already in Berceo, eighty years later. *Intacto*, the condition or appearance of many things at that hour, occurs eleven times; *persianas*, the window-blinds through which the light of morning is commonly if unromantically perceived, six times; and the *sombras*, shadows, which are driven away, come over thirty times. The light of early morning is often yellow, in Spain; and one might imagine, from the numerous occurrences of *amarillo*, *amarillear*, *amarillento*, *amarillez*—the word may be connected with 'pale'—that it was Guillén's favourite colour, for he uses it more than thirty times in his poetry. Yet this is not so; blue, azure (*azul*, *azulando*, *azulado*) is mentioned thirty-nine times; and green (*verde* and *verdor*) forty-one times. His order of preference for colours is, therefore: green, blue, yellow, white—almost the exact opposite of Antonio Machado whose order was: white, yellow, green, blue.[19] Among the colour-words which he remembers with most pleasure is *tornasol*: generally 'shot, iridescent', though it also brings a suggestion of the colour-changes undergone by litmus in the chemistry of our youth, and (to a lover of the old language) an obsolete word for the sunflower. Using it in the first sense, Guillén describes how the foreshortened

limbs of a girl bathing become confused with the iridescence of
the pebbles on the bed of the stream:

> Escorzo de piernas
> Tornasol de guijas.
>
> (*El manantial*)

Through the green sunblinds the greenness of the branches is all
a *tornasol*:

> Tras de las persianas
> Verdes, el verdor
> De aquella enramada
> Toda tornasol.
>
> (*Tornasol*)

Again, he asks whether the light is due to the siesta of a bird
whose colours are changing while it remains hidden:

> ¿Es tal vez una siesta con un pájaro
> Que se tornasola, recóndito?
>
> (*Hasta la sombra*)

Later, when dreaming of Spain from exile, reality seemed
nothing but a *tornasol* of the mind:

> Realidad, realidad
> En tornasol, en mente.
>
> (*Luz natal*)

There was also a Spanish sea-shell, he remembered, called
tornasol:

> Entre arenas los llaman
> Tornasoles amigos.
>
> (*Playa*)

Much of the early poetry was the poetry of waking up; and one
of the first objects beheld by the opening eye, was the *alero*, the
overhanging or projecting roof, so called because, from the begin-
nings of the Spanish language and in the natural imagery of its
earliest speakers, an overhanging roof suggested a wing, *ala*, and
was therefore called *alero*. It was always associated in the poet's
mind with other roofs; with clouds, distances:

> Un alero, tejados,
> Nubes allí, distancias
>
> (*Más allá*)

or with the leaves on the bough, the branches on the trunk, the
walls, the roofs, the corners, the posts:

> Las hojas en la rama, las rama en el tronco,
> Los muros, los aleros, las esquinas, los postes.
>
> (*Uns ventana*)

Or, again, with the window-boxes, the iron gratings, the corners:

> Los jardinillos, las verjas,
> Las esquinas, los aleros.
>
> (*El aire*)

So that in a mood of torrid helplessness, when even the pavement in the shade 'trembles wtih hidden bulls', the sun can be said to have *aleros*:

> ¡ Desampara tórrido !
> La acera de sombra
> Palpita con toros
> Ocultos. Y topan.
> Un sol sin aleros.
>
> (*El sediento*)

Another word for which Guillén has a curious fondness is *resbalar*, to slip or slide. There is the slipping-by of the morning compared to the slipping-by of the cars, up and down the avenue. (*Además.*) Days lengthen without boundaries, slipping-by

> ensanchos de días
> Sin lindes, resbalados.
>
> (*El distraído*)

The breeze slips between the vigorous rays of the sun (*Esfera terrestre*), and the light slides endlessly between its limits (*El horizonte*), along the paths (*Translación*), and over the shadow (*Amistad de las noche*).

Among the less common words used by Jorge Guillén are two concerned with noise and confusion. *Algazara* (found seven times) is an Arabic word which the Christians picked up from the Moslems; it has been firmly established in the language since the time of the oldest ballads. *Batahola* (five times) is an Italianism (*battagliola*) which came in during the sixteenth century as a nautical term: 'a place between the Oares of a galley where the souldiers did use to stand to fight',[20] and, by extension, the shouting which came from that place. Many of the poems, it was said, are like first waking up. 'The dawn! Everything's possible, even to-day.'

> ¡El alba! Todo me espera
> También hoy.
>
> (*Fe*)

'Dawn. The horizon half opens its eye-lashes and begins to see'

> Albor. El horizonte
> Entreabre sus pestañas
> Y empieza a ver.
>
> (*Los nombres*)

Milton said the same in *Lycidas*: 'Under the opening eyelids of the Morn'; but Guillén's horizon begins to see. What? Names. They are over the patina of things. The rose to-day is still called rose, and the memory of its passing, haste. Haste to live more.

> ¿Qué? Nombres.
> Están sobre la pátina
> De las cosas. La rosa
> Se llama todavía
> Hoy rosa, y la memoria
> De su tránsito, prisa.
>
> Prisa de vivir más.

'And the roses? Eyelashes shut; last horizon. Perhaps nothing? But there remain the names.'

> ¿Y las rosas? Pestañas
> Cerradas: horizonte
> Final. ¿Acaso nada?
> Pero quedan los nombres.

On another morning he writes: 'I feel the world beneath the day which restrains my eyelids. Well they hide me, my eyelashes':

> Siento el mundo bajo el día
> Que me embarga
> Los párpados. Bien me esconden
> Las pestañas.
>
> *(Alborada)*

Time circulates between hands of watches. Everything is saved in its circle; everything is round world (or 'roundness').

> Circula el tiempo entre agujas
> De relojes,
> Todo se salva en su círculo.
> Todo es orbe.

The omission of the article has surprised some critics; but Jorge Guillén is doing no more than George Meredith. In fact his relation to Meredith's nature poems is probably closer than his presumed relation to Whitman, not only in syntax but in feeling. 'Summit of delight! Everything in the air is bird!'

> ¡Cima de la delicia!
> Todo en el aire es pájaro.
>
> *(Cima de la delicia)*

But with other music, implacable employment of metal and
string, a world is created where there are never any dead.

> Implacable empeño
> De metal y cuerda;
> Un mondo se crea
> Donde nunca hay muertos
>
> (*Música, sólo música*)

Our morning, hardly future and always incognito:

> Nuestro mañana apenas
> Futuro y siempre incógnito.
>
> (*Salvación de la primavera*)

4

Jorge Guillén has written three times on the nature of poetry.
In a study of the poetry of Bécquer[21] he does his utmost to see poetry
through the eyes of Bécquer himself, collecting every expression of
Bécquer's opinion and giving Bécquer's mind without a word of
later events to distract us. Only in referring to Bécquer's avoidance
of rhetoric can we see that Guillén is telling us what he was able to
learn from the earlier poet himself.

The introduction to the Spanish translation and commentary of
The Song of Songs, made by Fray Luis de León for a nun who could
not read it in Latin, is a more personal expression of Jorge Guillén's
views.[22] The translation, Aubrey Bell and others have shown, was
the chief cause of Luis de León's arrest and confinement by the
Inquisition. It had been copied surreptitiously; copies multiplied,
and one of them even reached Peru, though there were believed
to be things in this canonical book of the Old Testament which
could only be permitted to sixteenth-century Spaniards in the decent
obscurity of a learned language.

Fray Luis ignored the allegorical interpretation and passed it by
without notice. For him, the book described the Arcadian loves
of a shepherd and a shepherdess. Large volumes, he said, had been
written by devout and holy men to penetrate the arcana of the
poem; but of the original meaning the previous commentators
had said little. Fray Luis, in his own exposition, kept strictly to the
literal meaning of the text, to what he called the bark of the written
word (*la corteza de la letra*), the surface (*sobrehaz*) and the sound
(*sonido*) without admitting that that outer covering did not agree

well with the 'meaning claimed by the Holy Ghost'. It was necessary, he thought, to say straight out what the significance of those
words was, in their outward and carnal sense, in order to understand their inward and spiritual application, but he did not wish to
say more than what they really meant. Learning, passion and
sensuality were united, Guillén concluded, in the person of a bookish
man who was both studious and ardent by temperament; they
increased his natural ardour in order to see more clearly, and the
words take fire and glow in the Spanish version of the *Song of Songs*
as they do in the English of the Authorized Version.

San Juan de la Cruz also derives from the *Song of Songs*, which,
under one form or another, had become an absolute necessity to
the tortured, repressed minds of Counter-Reformation Spain.
In his study of San Juan's poetry,[23] Guillén points out that poetry,
poesía, was a word which the saint never once used. He mentions
rhetoric, metaphor and style; but the only time that he employs the
word *poeta*, he applies it to the reputed author of the book of
Proverbs, Solomon.

A poet of any consideration always has his poetics—a *poética*, a
theory of poetry, more or less clear in his mind and more or less
distinctly formulated; a general view of the poetry which he has
already written and of that which he still hopes to write in the
future. Although San Juan de la Cruz never referred to poetry
by name, he left a complete theory of poetry in the Prologue to his
Cántico Espiritual. 'It is an admirable passage, proclaiming that
poetry is, in the last resort, ineffable. San Juan declares, directly or
indirectly, that love is the theme; but since it is inexpressible, a
partial attempt to convey the meaning may be made by recourse
to poetry; for imagery, metaphor and symbol (*figuras, compara-
ciones, semejanzas*) may suggest something of its secret mysteries.'
The language, of course, may overstep the limits of intelligibility,
'so that in the light of reason a *figura* will sound an absurdity (*dis-
late*), and therefore cannot be completely understood or entirely
explained'. The comprehension of a poem, or the ability to construe
it, is not everything; it does not give us the whole of its content.
'An essential ineffability goes with an essential unintelligibility.'

San Juan's commentary on his own poems, Guillén continues, is
given modestly without proposing to overshadow the text. Con-
sequently, every reader can enter at his ease by the open door of
the poetry: *los dichos de amor es mejor dejarlos en su anchura*. San
Juan had to invent a whole world of his own and then bring it to life

in words; from them his unspeakable intuition became objective
in imagery and rhythm. In the three great poems there is nothing
but imagery in irresistible rhythm; unreal but concrete representations which go to form a simple love-story. There is nothing abstract
about it. 'The action of the poem could hardly need less explanation. There is the lover and the beloved, and their transports of
passion; and the story is self-sufficing in nearly every line.'

What meaning, then, is hidden behind this miraculous poem?
'To begin with, there is the poem itself, with its near horizon, its
infinite distances, its poetic echoes. From the external world the
poet has imagined the flowery couch, *nuestro lecho florido*, and the
beloved becoming one with the lover, *amada en el amado transformada*;
but he attributes to motives of desire, *los bienes sensuales*, the whole
hidden mechanism of the imaginary conversation between the two
lovers, on which the plot of the poem is constructed.' Then there
are the *ninfas de Judea*, 'those historically hybrid creatures', who
symbolize 'all the imaginings, fancies, movements and affections
of the lower part of the soul'. There is also that García Lorca-
like idea, the gipsy of the senses, *el gitano del sentido*; and 'the waters,
airs, fires and fears that in the night are set to watch you':

> aguas, ayres, ardores,
> Y miedos de las noches veladores,

—grief, hope, fear, joy; images derived from concepts which can
be translated into abstract forms. Guillén hears the poet in San
Juan de la Cruz singing in terms human as well as divine, so that they
are enough, of themselves, to persuade the hearer and win him over.
The double, mystical allegorical meaning remains outside and
unnecessary, 'both anterior and posterior to the work itself and to
its own existence as a poem. San Juan explains nothing logically,
yet the whole poem is full of light'.

The main characteristic of San Juan de la Cruz is fluency; verse
flows from his pen with an ease unknown to Garcilaso and incon-
ceivable to Luis de León; the only poet with whom he can possibly
be compared in that respect is Lope de Vega. It is true that he
borrows extensively from *The Song of Songs*: imitates the form,
transplants the imagery and translates the words. But the *Cántico
Espiritual* would not be what it is (José María de Cossío has remarked)
without the popular Renaissance elements; it would only have been
one more biblical paraphrase, without grace or personality of its
own. San Juan de la Cruz affects neither the grand manner of

Herrera or the archaism of Luis de León, the means by which
these poets endeavoured to counterfeit the solemnity of the Bible;
yet he can produce effects of real solemnity steeped in popular
emotion. He can use the expression, already antiquated in his time,
acaba de entregarse ya de veras, a thought for which D. H. Lawrence
alone could have found an adequate rendering in English; or
stammer, with a naturalness which can only be genuine, *un no sé
qué que quedan balbuciendo*. He can write of *el robo que robaste*,
manage a diminutive like *montiña*, a verbal form like *perfumea*,
or an affectionate familiarity like *perdidiza*. 'These come from a
deliberate effort to be popular, and, by being popular, archaic; not
surely through intensive study, but through the imperative of a
living tradition which he has interpreted with insuperable felicity.'[24]

He borrows also from Renaissance platonism. The *amada en el
amado transformada* was already there, in a sonnet of Camoens:
Transforma-se o amador na cousa amada, which came originally from
Petrarch: *L'amante nell'amato si trasforma*. But it is the vivid, concentrated, telescopic phrases rather than the mysticism which have
fixed him in the affection of Jorge Guillén and all modern Spanish
poets: *leche de suauidad, el siluo de los ayres amorosos, la soledad sonora,
la música callada, ínsulas estrañas, valles solitarios, el ayre de tu buelo,
miedos de la noche veladores, lámparas de fuego, las profundas cauernas
del sentido*. . . . The power to invent musical phrases like these,
to create magical sounds out of simple Spanish words, made San
Juan de la Cruz the great Spanish poet that he is. 'We must',
Alfonso Reyes has wisely said, 'when it is a question of San Juan
de la Cruz, think only of the poetry . . . of the words most beautifully wrought that our language possesses.'[25] And Moreno Villa
speaks of 'the way he gives the words a transcendental brilliance. . . .
The words, typical of San Juan, are like flashes which light up two
landscapes at once, that of immediate reality and that of the other
reality which can only be suggested by the imagery of the former;
words which sometimes seem sheer magic and full of mystery,
and at other times almost too realistic.'[26]

'From the state of ineffability', Jorge Guillén adds, 'he leaps gaily
to the purest creation. San Juan de la Cruz has to invent for himself
a whole world incarnate in words; and those inexpressible intuitions
are made objective in the images of a rhythm. ¡*Soledad sonora*!
In the three great poems there is nothing but imagery: unreal yet
concrete representations which form the account of a love-affair.

Yet nothing abstract is mingled with the story, which is reduced
to the movements and emotions of a single pair of lovers.'

In his language, San Juan de la Cruz is probably the only Spanish
poet to have, besides his amazing fluency, 'that undiluted imaginative
richness' which we find in the great English poets. That may be the
reason why apologists in Spain imply that his poetry was written
by a divine hand; in England we know that Shakespeare, Milton
and Keats could write it themselves. San Juan honestly admits that
God gave him some of his verses, but that he had to find the rest
for himself—meaning that some were inspired, but others not.
Spanish poetry can do many things better than we can in English:
we have lost the language of popular speech, we have grown
ashamed of the rhetorical, and have never really achieved the
baroque; but we can certainly provide the 'simple, sensuous and
passionate language' which is the essence of the style of San Juan.
The source of that language, which he shares with the English
poets, is the Old Testament. It is shown fully only in four poems:
the four usually mentioned, *Cántico espiritual*, *Noche obscura*, *Llama
de amor viva* and the first few stanzas of *Que bien sé yo*. The language
of this poetry is certainly highly imaginative, sensually vivid and
intense. It can fairly and accurately be described as erotic, and
anthropomorphic; but it is doubtful whether it can claim to be—
like some of Blake, Wordsworth or Emily Brontë—poetry of
mystical experience.

Alas, that the currency of Spanish mysticism should have been so
debased! Mystical poetry in Spanish has been commercialized and
vulgarized like those exquisite Manila shawls which only Spanish
shoulders can wear, or like *cante jondo*, once so great a musical
experience in *carceleras* and *cartageneras* with Manuel de Falla, but
now an unbearable noise on the radio or gramophone.

5

Jorge Guillén is probably unbearable on another machine, the
machine of translation. It is possible that English may not have the
right kind of words or metres; but it is more likely that translators
have not yet discovered how to use English words for this particular
Spanish poet. A few specimens may illustrate some of the various
styles in which Jorge Guillén has written; but literal translation is

not enough. The essence of Spanish poetry is in the sound and rhythm of Spanish words.

DESPERTAR

Nada. Tinieblas muelles.
Y de un golpe . . . ¿Qué, quién?

Restauración por vértigo,
Brusca restauración en aquel bulto
Que estaba así negándose.
Dulcemente dormido.

Negándose. ¿Negado?
Por la memoria alboreada irrumpe,
Vertical y de súbito,
Una abertura hacia el vacío.
¿Es una sima?
Sima . . . ¿De dónde?
Aquel bulto se siente ser, no está.
Casí ahogándose cae, cae. ¿Cuándo?

Y una angustia, relámpago en albor,
illumina el olvido y su desierto.
El atónito cae, se detiene.

Yo. Yo ahora. Yo aquí.
Despertar, ser, estar:
Otra vez el ajuste prodigioso.

WAKING UP

Nothing. Darkness. Softness.
And on a sudden . . . Who's there?

Then restoration by giddiness.
Restoration, a rough jolt for that bulk
That lay there thus denying itself,
Blissfully unconscious.

Denying and denied?
Then through the morning memory, opens up,
sudden and rectilinear,
a wide-mouthed aperture upon the void.
Is it a cavern?
Cavern . . . where from?
That bulk feels it exists, but is not there.
almost drowning, and falling, falling. When?

And a feeling of fear, a lightning flash in the dawn
will illuminate the desert of forgetting.
The astounded being falls, and is stopped there.

I. I here and now.
Wide awake, existing, here now;
Once again, the marvellous adjustment.

LAS SOMBRAS

Sol. Activa persiana.
Laten sombras. ¿Quién entra?
. . . Huyen. Soy yo: pisadas.

(¡ Oh, con palpitación
De párpado, persiana
De soledad o amor !)

Quiero lo transparente.
También las sombras quiero,
Trasparentes y alegres.

(¡ Las sombras, tan esquivas,
Soñaban con la palma
De la mano en caricia !)

¿ Tal vez mi mano? Pero
No, no puede. Las sombras
Son intangibles: sueños.

THE SHADOWS

Sun. The fluttering sun-blind.
Shadows throbbing.—Who is it?
. . . Gone now. It's I: those footsteps.

(Oh, the tremble, so slight,
of an eyelid; window-blind
of loneliness or love !)

I like a thing transparent.
Again, I love the shadows.
Transparent and cheerful things.

(The shadows that so shyly
were dreaming of the spread palm
of a hand in a caress !)

Perhaps it's mine? But no,
It cannot be; for shades are
Intangible: mere dreams.

FRAGMENTS
Snow

Lo blanco está sobre lo verde
Y canta.
Nieve que es fina quiere
Ser alta . . .

The white lies over the green
And sings.
Snow that's so fine would be
Deep snow . . .

Early Morning

Todo el frío es un blanco:
Blanco en olor a verde.
¡ Qué leve
La calle bajo el cielo derramado !
Huele
Casi a manzana.
¡ Verdor agraz ! . . .

Everything cold is a white thing.
White with a smell of green.
How lightly
The street is strewn under the cold sky !
The scent
Almost like an orange
Green that's unripe ! . . .

Cierro los ojos

Cierro los ojos y el negror me advierte
Que no es negror, y alumbra unos destellos
Para darme a entender que sí son ellos
El fondo en algazara de la suerte,

Incógnita nocturna ya tan fuerte
Que consigue ante mí romper sus sellos
Y sacar del abismo los más bellos
Resplandores hostiles a la muerte.

Cierro los ojos. Y persiste un mundo
Grande que me deslumbra así, vacío
De su profundidad tumultuosa.

Mi certidumbre en la tiniebla fundo,
Tenebroso el relámpago es más mío,
En lo negro se yergue hasta una rosa.

I shut my eyes, and then the darkness tells me it's not quite dark; there's light from some faint sparkles, to make me understand that they are really the depth and cheering crowd to all my fortune.

That unknown thing by night, so strong already, will break through, in my presence, all that seals it; and draw up from the deep abyss the finest of splendours that still seem so far from death.

I shut my eyes. And there's a world still there, so great, it almost blinds me; but it's empty of that great other world's tumultuous depth.

My certainty is founded in the dark; darkened, the lightning seems more truly mine, and in black night there rises ever a rose.

NOTES

[1] Pedro Salinas, *Reality and the poet in Spanish Poetry* (Baltimore, 1940). He died in 1951. When we met for the last time—accidentally at Querétaro, in Mexico, in 1939—he had all the old friendliness, and the poet's clear vision of things to come.

[2] The infant Santo Domingo was *salteriado de hymnos e de cánticos* (*Vida*, 38); and after one of the miracles of Our Lady, all the clergy *ficieron un buen cántico*. *Milagros*, 452).

[3] Pedro Salinas, *Literatura española siglo XX*. (Mexico, 1941), p. 269, and 2 ed. (1949), p. 189.

[4] Theodora Bosanquet, *Paul Valéry* (1933), 52, 67.

[5] *Revista de Occidente*, XXIV, 1929, No. 72, pp. 340 ff. The English version by C. Day Lewis only appeared (*in Orion*) in 1945. What Guillén admired in Valéry, he says, was 'el esfuerzo exigente en la creación — y junto "esfuerzo" y "creación" — y el rigor en la forma'.

[6] *Cruz y Raya*, No. 11, Feb. 1934. The French original will be found in *Positions et Propositions*, II (Paris, 1934), pp. 67–88.

[7] *Poniente de bronce* (two romances): *Ventoleras y Circunloquios* (prose). One of the earliest poems published by Jorge Guillén is *Colores de un solo arco*, printed in the weekly review *España* for August 21, 1920 (año VI, núm. 277, p. 11). It has not been reprinted. In 1927 and 1928 he and a colleague in Murcia edited a review, *Verso y prosa*, which ran for twelve numbers, and contained contributions by Guillén and others.

[8] Dámaso Alonso. *Aquella arpa de Bécquer* in *Cruz y Raya*, No. 27, 1935; Guillén, *La poética de Bécquer*. (New York, 1943), p. 17. The saying, attributed to Antonio Machado, that the poetry of Bécquer was 'an accordion played by an angel' really came from Eugenio d'Ors.

[9] Angel del Río, in *Revista Hispánica Moderna*, IX, 4 (1943), pp. 315–317. See also R. Gullón and J. M. Blecua, *La poesía de Jorge Guillén. Dos ensayos* (Saragossa, 1946) and E. M. Wilson, in *Atlante*, 1 (1953).

[10] Letter to Fernando Vela (1926) quoted in Gerardo Diego, Poesía española; Antología 1913–31 (Madrid, 1932 and 1934).

[11] F. Porché, *Paul Valéry et la poésie pure*. (Paris, 1926), pp. 7–8. See also Alfonso Reyes, *Mallarmé entre nosotros* (Mexico, 1955).

[12] *Variété, II*, 13 ed. (1930), pp. 155–156.

[13] Frances Pleak, *The Poetry of Jorge Guillén* (Princeton, 1942).

[14] Américo Castro, ''Cántico' de Jorge Guillén In *Insula* (Buenos Aires) 1943, I, No. 1. E. R. Curtius, *La poesía de Jorge Guillén* in *Insula* (Madrid), No. 73, Enero, 1952, sensibly points out that Guillén's poetry is an expression which is sufficient to itself; it has no need of any philosophical commentary, though it can serve a philosopher as a text for meditation. He shows the importance of the early prose piece, *Aire-Aura*, in *Revista de Occidente* (Madrid) No. 4, Oct. 1933.

[15] J. Casalduero, *Jorge Guillén: Cántico*. (Santiago de Chile, 1946.)

[16] *Leyendo* (El Colegio de Mexico, 1944).

[17] Amado Alonso and Pedro Henríquez Ureña, *Gramática Castellana*, 2° curso. (Buenos Aires, 1939) — 159–165.

[18] *Mélange* (Toronto, 1941), p. 49.

[19] H. Jeschke, *Die Generation von 1898 in Spanien*. (Halle, 1934), 76.

[20] Minsheu, *Vocabularium hispanico-latinum et anglicum. A most copious Spanish dictionarie* (1617?), and Terlingen, *Los italianismos en español* (1943).

21 *La Poesía de Bécquer.* (Hispanic Institute, New York, 1943).

22 Luis de León, *Cantar de Cantares*, edición y prólogo de Jorge Guillén. (Madrid, 1936).

23 *San Juan de la Cruz y la poesía*, in *Revista de las Indias*, Bogotá, núm. 50, Feb. 1943.

24 José María de Cossío, *Rasgos renacentistas y populares en el Cántico Espiritual. Escorial*, Nov. 1942, 205–228.

25 Alfonso Reyes, *Trazos de historia literaria* (2 ed., Buenos Aires-Mexico, 1951), pp. 134–135.

26 J. Moreno Villa, *Leyendo* . . . (1944), pp. 12–13. An English admirer of the Saint has curiously described his poetry as 'a cooling draught of heaven-brewed Spanish ale'.

There have been four editions of the *Cántico* of Jorge Guillén: 1. Revista de Occidente, Madrid, 1928 (75 poems); 2. Cruz y Raya, Madrid, 1936 (125 poems); 3. Litoral, Mexico, 1945 (270 poems); 4. Editorial Sudamericana, Buenos Aires, 1950 (334 poems). Subsequent to these are *Variaciones sobre temas de Jean Cassou*, Mexico, 1951, the essay on Salinas, *Profesión y oficio*, in *Número* Año 4, No. 18: Montevideo, 1952, and *Huerto de Melibea*, in *Inventario*, Anno 5, N. 1–4: Milan, 1953.

H

VI

CERVANTES

I

FROM the north shore of the Gulf of Corinth—from the tiny
port of Naupactus or Lepanto near which Cervantes lost the
use of one hand—the traveller has a view across the water to the
actual, geographical Arcadia. The grandeur, the remote beauty of
the piled mountain mass is surprising, unexpected; the names on
the map are a passage from a world of fact-finding to a realm of pure
poetry. Erymanthus and Cyllene are not mere literary expressions,
but dreams come true; the river Styx is a little stream falling over a
precipice.

Life in the Peloponnesian Arcadia must always have been hard:
far from any condition likely to favour the shepherds and
shepherdesses of an 'Arcadian' pastoral novel. Ovid thought the
Arcades beastly in their habits; Juvenal took them for types of
primitive stupidity. Yet a sober historian like Polybius considered
that the real Arcadians must have been humanized by the law
compelling them to learn music; and, with Cervantes, the ideal
Arcadia must be taken seriously if he is to be read at all. Don
Quixote has much to say about it; while in the first novel, *La
Galatea*, a number of 'Arcadian' shepherds discuss their private
affairs in an urbane and civilized manner according to Platonic
conventions, and then make poetry about them. It is, in fact, a
novela poemática—to borrow the title given to some of his earlier
stories by Pérez de Ayala a generation ago.

We cannot afford (though some critics do so) to pass by *La
Galatea*; Cervantes himself was too fond of it. Living when he did,
in the first century of the Spanish Empire and at the beginning of
the *Contrarreforma*, the Counter-Reformation, we might have
expected to see him blowing the trumpet of universal empire or
swinging the censer of world-wide ecclesiastical authority. But we
do not. What we actually find is a tolerant, disillusioned man,
always ready to help or sympathize with people younger than himself. Cervantes may have thought that Platonic love was an overrated amusement. He may have thought that the other sort of

love was an overrated amusement too. But he never got in the way of people who did not think so, or who had not yet reached the age of thinking so. He always took younger people very seriously; and it was only their elders (when experience might have made them wiser), whom he regarded as subjects for comedy. Cervantes had knocked about the world a good deal—and had been knocked about by the world a good deal; and his own experience cannot have been very different from that of the old witch, La Cañizares, near the end of the last Exemplary Novel: *El Coloquio de los perros* (The dogs' debate). She is describing how she was imprisoned and flogged by the police; but she goes on:

Pero esto ya pasó, y todas las cosas se pasan; las memorias se acaban, las vidas no vuelven, las lenguas se cansan, los sucesos nuevos hacen olvidar los pasados.

But that has gone by, and all things go by, memories fade, lives do not return, tongues grow tired, and new events make us forget what is past.

This tolerant, sympathetic, kindly, middle-aged man always had an affection for his first book, *La Galatea*, and always wanted to bring out a sequel to it in spite of its dependence on the pastoral convention. Unlike most of his critics Cervantes did not think that convention absurd; and we shall never understand him properly unless we try to see that the pastoral convention had something else in it than absurdity.

To begin with, Cervantes was not so young when he embarked on his pastoral novel; in 1585 when it was published he was thirty-seven. We might have expected him to be a thoroughly disillusioned man. He had come back, five years before, from being a prisoner of war in Algiers. He was an unsuccessful dramatist and poet; he had had an affair with an actress, and was responsible for an illegitimate daughter. He had known the seamy side of town life, and his experiences of the country were far from ideal. He had fallen violently for a village-maiden at Illescas, whom he may first have seen in the gorgeous village costume of the province of Toledo. He married her, and she brought him a small dowry including twenty-five hens and a rooster; but her family of hard-headed, well-to-do farmers or small landowners, had no use for a writing man, and least of all for an ex-service man out of employment. They did their best to tie up the property so that Cervantes should not run through it; and, for years, he and his country wife lived apart. She was not there, for instance, when the police raided his house at Valladolid in 1605, after a dying man had been found on the doorstep. Cervantes' contacts with the country had not been

exactly Arcadian, or according to the pastoral convention. He knew
enough about the country to realize that real country-people are
very different from the characters in a pastoral novel; and in *El
coloquio de los perros* he makes the sheep-dog explain to the other
that the life of a real shepherd is very different from that of a
shepherd in Arcadia. Cervantes, unlike some of his modern critics,
never confused the two kinds of shepherd.

La Galatea is a *novela pastoril*, not a *novela ejemplar*; a book of prose
and poetry in which we find what Cervantes called *cosas soñadas y
bien escritas*—things dreamed of and well written—a deliberately
artificial form, intended for a society which had just been presented
with the greatest empire the world had ever seen, and yet—in spite
of that or because of that—was turning away from reality to *cosas
soñadas y bien escritas*: a people essentially rationalistic, humorous
and unsentimental, deliberately dreaming a world of imagination
—a world as unreal as the world of Don Quixote's mind. It was
true that for the entertainment of the idle there were also books of
chivalry, *libros de caballerías*. They were not particularly well
written; they were only thought fit for pages and waiting-women.
Cervantes, though he devoured books of chivalry himself, made
fun of enchanted castles and chivalry, with their giants and dwarfs
and magicians; but he never made fun of Arcadia or the pastoral
convention, for which he had only a grave smile.

In a book of chivalry, a critic has remarked, everything is decided
by force; in a pastoral novel, the chief weapons are words and
poems and musical instruments. The Arcadian shepherd, by speaking well, achieves as much as the knight-errant by cutting off
the heads of dragons and giants. In the one, it is all action; in the
other, all talk. That is too sweeping a statement. In the books of
chivalry not everything is force; in the pastoral novel not everything is talk, and least of all in the *Galatea*, which begins with a
murder followed by bandits and storms at sea and naval engage-
ments, all drawn from the recollections of Cervantes himself.
What a difference there is between Cervantes' *Galatea* and the
Arcadia of Lope de Vega! There we find terrific giants, involved
with nymphs of Diana who fail to keep their vows of chastity
and are changed by the goddess into mountains where they bring
forth shepherds; huge palaces with the prophetic history of Spanish
grandees inscribed on their marble walls. In *La Galatea* we have a
select world of shepherds with invariable good manners, who never
assert themselves or push themselves forward, and who behave

(an Italian critic says)[1] as if they were friends of La Rochefoucauld in seventeenth-century France; and shepherdesses who, without being exactly *précieuses ridicules*, are always *discretas y comedidas*.

Pastoral romance was classical in the French sense; and classical, too, in the sense of the unchanging conditions of life in the country—the only form of existence which had a long and unbroken continuity with the ancient world. Pastoral romance was Mediterranean. It stood for everything that was classical in opposition to what was medieval and 'gothick', and more particularly, in opposition to the strange ideology of medieval chivalry. In contrast to the stormy, restless life of the medieval knight-errant, the *novela pastoril* brought the quiet life of the man who had plenty of time for everything, and never had to do anything in a hurry; a man of speculation rather than of action, 'a man of words and not of deeds', a man who was repelled by the *aventurero* and *arrivista*, and the tiresome individual who is always trying to remake the world by the affirmation of his own personality.

'Pastoral' is not merely the young poet, Cardenio, suffering the circumstances of his own tragedy and taking refuge in the wilderness; nor is it only Marie-Antoinette playing with classicism at the Petit Trianon and masquerading as a shepherdess. The pastoral novel represented the effects of reason, culture and poetry, which alone could make life in a civilized society prevail over the life of the instinct. If we think of the *caballero del verde gabán* (the man in the green cloak) in the Second Part of *Don Quixote*, we realize that the pastoral ideal is very like the ideal which he, too, possessed; the man in the green cloak is an Arcadian shepherd who has married and settled down.

Pastoral poetry goes back to Hesiod. He was 'the shepherd who had seen the Muses', who had found them at the foot of Mount Helicon and learnt from them songs which were above the gross, material life of earth; and the enchanting prelude to his Theogony began not only didactic, agricultural poetry but pastoral poetry as well. There may seem little resemblance between Hesiod and Theocritus; still less between him and Virgil; but there are connexions, and Virgil sometimes says clearly what Hesiod, through uncertainty or timidity, was unable to express. We find in him the idea of a pastoral Arcadia, a country where poetry is natural; and it was this that particularly appealed to poets of the Renaissance.[2]

With Theocritus in the Greek colonies of Sicily, the shepherds—naturalistic as they are—do not often seem real shepherds. (His

fishermen sound real, but not his shepherds.) The same is true of
Virgil: the real shepherds, or at least the real country people, hardly
come into the *Eclogues*; though now and again, at the end of an
eclogue, we hear the voice of a real countryman making a real
country remark. It is as if, on a glorious morning in England, you
saw a countryman with a prize heavy-draught cart-horse; and then
heard him remark—as I did once—after contemplating the prospect
with evident satisfaction: 'Gee up, Rosie, yer b——!' In other
places in Virgil, in the *Georgics*, there are real shepherds occasionally,
though they are not near Virgil's home, but far away in the deserts
of Libya or the plains of Scythia, North Africa or Central Asia;
while his shepherdesses or country wenches are most alive when he
describes them sitting round a smoking lamp, carding wool on a
winter evening and seeing bad weather coming when the oil
sputters round the wick. But in Virgil there is one thing which
came later to many Spaniards: the melancholy pleasure of looking
back when driven off the land after a civil war; looking back
longingly, nostalgically, to a golden age; an Arcadia of patriarchal
customs. Yet many shepherds in Virgil and Theocritus are already
'Arcadians'; they are townsmen in a pastoral disguise.

The pastoral ideal represented something opposed to the world
of big business and imperial politics, both in Virgil's Italy and
Cervantes' Spain: it was a world of sheer poetry. In Spain, the
pastoral ideal looked back to some of the earliest poetry in the
Peninsula: to the groups of girls dancing and singing in medieval
Galicia, about the *flores do verde pino*, of *meu amado* and *meu amigo*;
or else dancing round the maypole or the *árbol de amor* in Castille,
and singing lines that run like limericks:

> A aquel árbol que mueve la hoja
> Algo se le antoja.

Those were originally pagan dances, fertility rites; and Arcadia
has been described by the historian of Italian literature, Francesco
de Sanctis, as 'sensuality ennobled by culture', 'the lonely kingdom
of art in the quiet and idyllic mind'.

The origins of pastoral in Spain, then, were not like French *fêtes
champêtres* (they turned into something like that afterwards) but
Spanish *fiestas de mayo*. From these, their descent can be traced
through the Archpriest of Hita, parodying the idyllic shepherdesses
in a gross, realistic manner in his *serranas*; and the exquisite, Don-
Juanesque *serranillas* of the Marqués de Santillana, which might

have been sung by Mozart's Don Giovanni to the village maiden Zerlina. There are realistic shepherds in Juan del Encina; but Juan del Encina was already a humanist, a pupil of Nebrija who, before writing his own eclogues, had begun by translating and adapting the eclogues of Virgil. In one of these, the situation is like that in Cervantes' exemplary novel, *La Gitanilla*: a townsman is attracted by a shepherdess and seeks to become a shepherd himself; and there are, of course, the Christmas shepherds, acted by townsmen in a realistic manner, in the plays of Juan del Encina and Gil Vicente. Yet the first Spanish pastoral poets, in the strict sense, were Boscán and Garcilaso; while the *Cántico espiritual* of St. Juan de la Cruz may fairly be described as a pastoral poem, like its Hebrew original, *The Song of Songs*. The first man in Spain to write a pastoral novel in dialogue form bore the sinister name of Torquemada, though he was not the great inquisitor himself. In 1553 he published a satirical *Coloquio pastoril* on the Italian model, the prose dialogue being interrupted by letters and poems, and ending with the three shepherds singing a trio. Then came Jorge de Montemayor (who was really Portuguese); and by the time of his *Diana* (1559), the *novela pastoril* was firmly founded in the Peninsula. This had come originally from Italy (like the forms of Garcilaso's poetry) with the *Arcadia* (1502) of Sannazaro. Sannazaro was a Neapolitan but of Spanish extraction; he had a Catalan Aragonese ancestor on the wrong side of the blanket. Though not the work of a poet of the first rank, his pastoral novel swayed the whole of Europe. The lyrical and poetical passages are really dramatic eclogues; and in Italy, the style developed into so exquisite a masterpiece as Tasso's *Aminta*—which probably suggested Don Quixote's speech to the goat-herds on the Golden Age. In the Peninsula Sannazaro's first pupil was the Portuguese Bernardim Ribeiro, whose pastoral romance *Menina e moça* gave the idea to Montemayor.

The shepherds of Juan del Encina and Gil Vicente were as realistic as actors could make them, both in speech and action; in their rough country dialects and their rude, pointed gestures. But the shepherds of Garcilaso, Montemayor and Cervantes—and even more, those of Sannazaro—were in no sense realistic; they were a creation of the intellect. With Cervantes, who was almost incapable of imagining men or women who had not something earthy in their composition, the shepherds and shepherdesses, the *pastores* and *pastoras*, belong to an ideal world of pure poetry, 'full of echoes of Plato'.[3] They were not, and were never meant to be, real shepherds;

they were courtiers (or, at any rate, educated people) masquerading as shepherds.

To us moderns of to-day, who have lost the classical enthusiasm of the Renaissance humanists, the pastoral novel may seem conventional and artificial; but to condemn sixteenth-century pastoral from a modern standpoint, shows an utter lack of historical sense. To the sensibility of the twentieth century, a pastoral novel may seem completely dead; but to the sensibility of the sixteenth century it was as alive as anything else. Its object was to give a vision of the perfect life. Garcilaso, in one of his sonnets, describes Nature as a strange idea and one not yet seen in the world:

una estraña y no vista al mundo idea;

while, according to Cervantes, Nature was *el mayor-domo de Dios*: God's butler. The belief in a happy 'state of Nature', in the remote past, was derived partly, no doubt, from the Bible story of the age of the patriarchs, but mainly from the classical myth of the Golden Age. That first age of man had not yet come to be regarded (as it had been by Lucretius and was later, in the seventeenth century by Hobbes) as one in which there was war of all against all, and life was 'nasty, brutish and short'.

It has become a commonplace of criticism, with some who have studied Modern Languages here and in America, to take a patronizing or contemptuous view of Spanish and Portuguese writers of the sixteenth century on account of their debt to classical Rome and Renaissance Italy.[4] That is an ill-informed view. Plagiarism? To call it that, is to misunderstand what people in those days thought; and it is still true that the greatest genius is the most indebted man. To writers and readers, in the time of the Renaissance, imitation of the ancients was less a right than a duty. By imitation or plagiarism, learned works were embellished with ornament and decoration, as if they were new buildings adorned with columns taken from a ruined temple or mouldings in the same style; and this was what happened with the pastoral romances.

It does not matter that the shepherds and shepherdesses are always described as feeding their flocks, with no connexion with the realities of a shepherd's life, which is hard enough, even in England to-day: 'lambing' on the South Downs has always been a chilly and anxious business for the shepherd. The only reference to that in *La Galatea* gives the impression that flocks multiplied naturally, and that lambs came into the world without any need for care or expert knowledge on the part of the shepherd. The truth is, that to speak of 'feeding flocks' is speaking figuratively, like Milton in that great poem in the pastoral convention: *Lycidas*. When Milton says that Lycidas and himself had been 'nurst upon the self-same hill, Fed the same flock, by fountain, shade and rill', he means that they were both at Cambridge, at the same time, and at the same College, and probably sharing the same rooms. When he says further that 'we drove afield, and both together heard What time the gray-fly winds his sultry horn, Batt'ning our flocks on the fresh dews of night', he means that they went to the same lectures, which began earlier than they do now. 'Meanwhile the rural ditties were not mute' refers to music—to music made among friends; for in those days there were no concerts, either in the England of Milton or the Spain of Cervantes, and the only music made in Arcadia was private music in which the performers were the shepherds themselves.

2

So then, a book describing an ideal society, where women are on an equality with men, centuries before that was so in ordinary life, ought not to be dismissed as childish. Here, in this ideal society, we find people not only figuratively feeding their flocks but telling stories, singing songs and discussing a variety of questions: particularly literature, music and philosophy—not exactly childish or negligible occupations.

These, in fact, became the normal occupations of the Arcadian academies in Italy in the seventeenth and eighteenth centuries.[5] The Arcadian academies realized some of the ideals of the Arcadian shepherds; members were known by names like those which we find in the *Galatea* and were held to be on an equality with one another, while women also had the right to membership. The existence of these academies had important practical consequences; a member going to live in another town was promptly received into one of the academies there and made to feel at home. One of the more curious consequences, however, was the attitude adopted by the Spanish authorities in those parts of Italy which they occupied. The Academy of the Animosi of Cremona, for instance,[6] was required to elect a new President every year, and to arrange that from time to time one of the members gave a lecture on the Spanish conception of honour. The object was to instruct members how to settle their differences on Christian principles, and live in peace without the perpetual menace of quarrels and murders. It is most interesting to see how the sense of honour formed an integral part of Spanish civilization overseas, so that, even in a country with so old a tradition of civilization as Italy, the Spanish government disposed that so important a thing as the sense of honour should not be forgotten, and the ideal of 'Arcadia' was one of the means by which this was accomplished.

The real occupations of the people in a pastoral novel are poetry, music and philosophical discussion. First, the poetry. Cervantes was a writer of prose rather than poetry; and there are better poems in other pastoral novels, particularly in the *Diana* of Montemayor and the *Diana enamorada* of Gaspar Gil Polo. Yet not all the poems of Cervantes are so negligible as the historians of Spanish literature would have us believe. The lines *Es el amor principio del bien nuestro*,[7] spoken by Tirsi, are, like many poems of the Spanish sixteenth century, full of ideas from Plato. Another poem of the same kind is the one in the third book: the lines beginning with the second stanza—Cervantes often does not find his feet until the second stanza—*Amor que es virtud entera*, sung by Elicio;[8] and the same is true of the lines in the fourth book sung by Lauso: *Tus ojos son, de cuya luz serena*,[9] lines which might almost have been written by Herrera. They belong, at any rate, to the same poetical world as the private, personal poems of Herrera, distinct from his public utterances like the three poems in the *Oxford Book of Spanish Verse*; and Cervantes belongs also to the world of Garcilaso and many of the sixteenth-century poets who followed him. It comes from Italy and is part of the poetical world of Petrarch and Michelangelo,[10] and the last few pages of *Il Cortigiano*, the splendid dialogue by Castiglione which was translated into Spanish by Boscán—into Spanish prose which set the standard for Spain all through the sixteenth century. Love has wings; is fired by beauty. Modern people can say that too, in a modern way: 'He shot me down in flames' an A.T.S. was overheard to remark to a friend in the middle of the late war, and it is an expression which, if not poetry, is something very like it. At the same time, with a poet who is platonizing, reason is put on its guard: *enciende el corazón y lo refrena* (can set the heart afire, then rein it in). Herrera said that, when emending a line in a sonnet of Garcilaso, or rather inserting a line of his own, instead of the one which Garcilaso had originally

written: *con clara luz la tempestad serena* (and with clear light make
stormy skies serene); trying to bar the way to mere appetite by
the light of intelligence.

This is not platonic love; it is reasoning about love in a platonic
manner, the manner of all the sixteenth-century Spanish poets who
were any good, including Cervantes and even S. Juan de la Cruz.
It does not mean that they were not passionate. On the contrary.
But it does mean that they had invented a language for talking
about their feelings, a language which was more expressive and
more poetic (if less scientifically, psycho-analytically accurate)
than the language of repressions and sublimations to which we have
grown accustomed; and that is what Cervantes' *Galatea* is really
about. In their discussions, the characters—the 'shepherds' and
'shepherdesses'—are occupied with what was one of the burning
questions of the day, a question which they knew concerned every
one of them, and one which the writings of a mysterious Spanish (or
Portuguese) exile living in Italy had placed in an entirely new light.
If Cervantes had been living a few years ago, he would have made
his *pastores* and *pastoras* discuss psycho-analysis and the theories of
Freud. Were he writing now, he might have made them discuss
existentialism and the works of Sartre. Writing, as he was, between
1583 and 1585, he made them discuss the platonic theory of love and
the ideas of Cardinal Bembo and León Hebreo. The comparison
is exact or exact enough. Platonic love, or rather, platonic theories
about love, held among those people a place equivalent to, or
comparable with, the place that psychology and psycho-analysis
do with us; and if one wants to see whether the shepherds are
talking sense or nonsense, one way of doing it would be to translate
their remarks (or think their remarks) into the language of psycho-
analysis.

There is a passage in *Persiles y Segismunda*[11] and certain places in
Don Quixote—above all where the shepherdess Marcela affirms her
right as a woman to lead her own life, like that other shepherdess,
Camila, in the second Eclogue of Garcilaso. But it is in *La Galatea*
that Cervantes expounds the Renaissance platonic theory of love,
or makes the shepherds expound it. One should remember that the
very name of Plato was something new in Renaissance times: new
and fashionable; and that, more effectively than Ficino, Bembo,
Castiglione, Equicola, Betussi or Tullia d'Aragona, León Hebreo
had modernized the Renaissance interpretation of love according

to Plato. The *Diálogos de amor* are definitely mentioned by Cervantes himself in the Prologue to the First Part of Don Quixote:

Si tratáredes de amores, con dos onzas que sepáis de la lengua toscana, toparéis con León Hebreo, que os hincha las medidas.

If love be your subject, with your two ounces of Tuscan you will meet with León Hebreo, who will satisfy you to your heart's content.

The reference may be ironical. Cervantes does not say that he has read León Hebreo himself; the evidence is rather that, if he had read the first book of León Hebreo, he had also read Bembo and Castiglione. Later he made Don Quixote recite a madrigal of Bembo's from *Gli Asolani*, one that was well known and set to music: *Quand' io penso al martire* — *Cuando las penas miro* is the Spanish translation.[12]

As a matter of fact it had not been necessary for Cervantes' readers to struggle with León Hebreo in Italian. There were two translations into Spanish already (1568 and 1584); while in 1590 a third and beautifully written translation was published—a translation which, in its period, is as great an achievement as Boscán's translation of *Il Cortigiano* two generations earlier. Its title is:

La traduzión del Indio de los tres Diálogos de Amor de León Hebreo, hecha de Italiano en Español por Garcilasso Inga de la Vega, natural de la gran Ciudad de Cuzco, cabeça de los reynos y provincias del Pirú.

Could anything be more Spanish than that: a book by an exile from Portugal and Spain, probably written in Italian, and translated into Spanish by a native of Peru! This admirable version has been reprinted in modern times;[13] but in its own day, because of the honesty of the translator and the integrity of the writer, the new version was soon placed on the *Index*.

The book is a long discussion—or rather, three long discussions—between two lovers, Philón and Sophía. Sophía is the quick, alert pupil, asking acute and intelligent questions; Philón is the master, the tutor, resolving all Sophía's doubts and answering all her objections. There is something of Abelard and Heloïse in the relationship; it is impossible to agree with Menéndez y Pelayo that the speakers are entirely abstract: *personajes enteramente abstractos que simbolizan, como sus nombres lo indican, el amor o el apetito, y la ciencia o sabiduría.* Their relative positions in the dialogue make that impossible; Sophía is definitely less learned than Philón, though her wits are sharper and her vision clearer.[14]

There were two other books, two other dialogues, which had the advantage of putting Platonic views of love more clearly and more shortly than León Hebreo, and with more point and humour. Both were translated into Spanish, and there was also a third dialogue, which, though written in Italian seems never to have been translated into Spanish, though the author was said to be the daughter of a Spanish cardinal: *Dell' infinita d'amore* (1547). Her name was Tullia d'Aragona, a lady of charm and learning and a good poet, but one whose favours were somewhat expensive. *Gli Asolani* (*Los Asolanos* in Spanish) by Cardinal Bembo (1505) is a lively discussion between three men and three women, in a garden on the mainland near Venice. Menéndez y Pelayo is unfair to it; it is much more alive than he would have us believe. *Il Cortigiano* (1516) of Baldassare Castiglione, is the account of several evenings' talk at the palace of the Duke of Urbino. It is by no means all taken up with platonic discussions about love; there is one discourse (which reminds one of *Don Quixote*) on the relative merits of arms and letters; but the last two chapters (or books) are a platonic consideration on love, and they are the most important part of the whole dialogue. In them, the chief speaker is the author of the other dialogue mentioned: Cardinal Bembo of *Gli Asolani*. The rest is a discussion of the ideal of the cultured man: what the cultured man should be, in his relations with men, women, ideas, music, and the world in general. There are several women taking part in the dialogue, and they express themselves with great spirit and frankness, including the young duchess herself; indeed, one cannot help feeling that she encouraged the conversation, and urged the talkers to continue far into the night, to keep them out of mischief. 'If', an Italian scholar wrote, 'Platonism could give so good an account of itself in the splendid yet brutal society of the Renaissance, that was because those ideas were so attractively expressed. Earthly love, now shown to be an incarnation of eternal verities, came to add yet one more splendour to that splendid life; the confusion between beauty and intellect flattered a society which was proud of its recovery of reason; and in the end, a gleam of philosophy seemed to light up even the medieval poetry of Petrarch with classicism.'[15]

Platonism, derived from Bembo, Castiglione and León Hebreo, played a considerable part in the pastoral world of Cervantes. Though the dialogue of León Hebreo is obviously conducted indoors, in the intimate surroundings of a study, both Bembo and Castiglione have something Arcadian in their surroundings.[16] In the fourth book of *La Galatea* we find *pastores* and *pastoras*—not real ones, of course, but shepherds and shepherdesses of Arcadia—who have gone to picnic, and *tener la siesta*, at a place called La Fuente de las Pizarras. To their surprise, they find people there already; but the strangers beg the shepherds not to run away: they cannot help remarking that the life of a shepherd in Arcadia seems to suit them. After a time, the discussion turns into a dispute between the *desamorado* Lenio who has been reading Bembo, and Tirsi who is full of León Hebreo. For Lenio, the whole thing is desire: that is all there is to be said for it; while Tirsi distinguishes between the love that is merely desire and that which (to quote the Catechism) is 'temperance, soberness and chastity'.

It is a misunderstanding of the whole situation to dismiss these discussions as the platonic loves of Arcadian shepherds. In fact, beneath their pastoral disguise, they behave like real men and women, who are not talking about 'platonic' love but about their own affections, reasoning about their affections in a platonic manner. There had been much that was not strictly 'platonic' (in the usual sense of the word) in the loves of Pietro Bembo and Lucrezia Borgia; she was one of the most beautiful women of her time, and at the height of his passion Bembo had written poems to her in Spanish or copied them out of one of the *Cancioneros*.[17] Yet his discussion, his reasoning on the subject of human affection, as it appears in the last pages of *Il Cortigiano*, is a most moving and beautiful piece of writing; and, in the translation by Boscán, it shows Castilian prose at one of its highest points.

It is true, as Menéndez y Pelayo said, that for many of the poets and men of letters, Platonism became little else than a collection of ready-made phrases and commonplaces: e.g. *el sumo Bien, unión en Dios*. It was, in fact, a form of rhetoric which came to be used too much, like the clichés of mysticism in certain schools of Spanish to-day. But for Herrera, the poet, who had thought deeply about these things, the language of Platonism and of poetry was not merely *una cristalización en formas regulares y muertas*, but *agua que eternamente fluye y se mueve*; and we ought, he insists (in his *Anotaciones a las obras de Garcilaso*)

debemos procurar con el entendimiento modos nuevos y llenos de hermosura.

Seek out with the understanding. Herrera puts us on the right lines once more; for there has been too much loose talk about mysticism, and not enough about philosophy. But here we must be on our guard too; for where so many modern critics go wrong is in treating the work of Cervantes as philosophy when it is really fiction. In the discussion in *La Galatea*, just as in many of the discussions in *Don Quixote*, we have a number of people discussing something in a novel; and since we are dealing with a novel and not with a text-book of philosophy, what is more important, even, than the ideas expressed, is that the conversation should be natural and alert. Considering the reputation of *La Galatea* for being un-readable—especially among those who have never seriously tried to read it—it is surprising how easily it runs.

Lenio (we have said) uses the arguments of Bembo rather than of León Hebreo; there is one passage straight from *Gli Asolani*, and two others which seem like clear reminiscence.[18] He states the case against love affairs, and Cervantes deliberately makes him overstate it, so as to give more chance to Tirsi, who follows with the ideas of León Hebreo—and gives, in fact, something like a lecture on them.

Yet, as we know, *La Galatea* is a work of fiction, not a text-book of philosophy, and we are entitled to look for naturalness in the dialogue; indeed this philosophical episode in a novel of Cervantes should be regarded in the same way as a philosophical episode in one of the Cambridge novels of E. M. Forster: *The longest journey*. In that novel, undergraduates are sitting round the fire in college rooms after tea; sitting in the dark and discussing a problem of elementary metaphysics: whether a cow which you see is really there. The point of it is not whether E. M. Forster is making a serious contribution to metaphysics and the theory of knowledge, but whether, as a novelist, he conveys the idea of undergraduates in Cambridge, fifty years ago, sitting round the fire after tea in the dark, discussing whether the cow is really there. A novelist writing of Cambridge to-day would probably have made people in those circumstances discuss being 'abroad', or music, or existentialism or the ideas of Lord Russell. Forster makes someone burst into the room and turn on the light, 'revealing' (as he says) 'the philosophers in curious attitudes'. Cervantes comes at the beginning of novel-writing, and is, of course, three hundred years behind E. M. Forster in technique; but he gets the novelist's effect by making the *pastores* and *pastoras* go off to picnic at the Fuente de las Pizarras, and find (when they get there) that others have got there first. Another novelist's effect—one of those little touches which can make a novel come to life—is that, at that very moment, just when Lenio was preparing to say abusive things about love-affairs, there arrived . . . none other than the lovely Galatea herself.

It can hardly be said that *La Galatea* is a good novel; but it is a novel, and it is as a novel that it should be judged, not as a statement of the platonic theory of love. There is much of the later Cervantes in it: a great deal of adventure at sea, and adventure of rather a different kind on land; accounts of what happened to people travelling to Barcelona or Naples; the experience of a man who was captured by bandits, and then believed by the police to be a bandit himself, arrested and almost executed. The book is full of comings and goings, the discomfort and unexpectedness of travel as it actually was in Spain and Italy in the time of Cervantes.

With all these, *La Galatea* should not be condemned because it is set in an artificial, Arcadian society of *pastores* and *pastoras*; for after all (as already said) we still have artificial societies to-day—and it is as natural for the persons in the *Galatea* of Cervantes to discuss platonic theories of love as it is for the persons in a modern novel to discuss surrealism or psycho-analysis. The echoes of Plato and the sound of Arcadian bagpipes are not so remote from us as some commentators would have us believe.

It is not altogether fanciful—and it has been done before—to see, in Virgil's first Eclogue, not two silly shepherds but two sophisticated Romans, at the end of the Civil War. They are heavily disguised in the 'pastoral' manner, and 'married to immortal verse' in some of the most exquisite lines that have ever been written; but we can recognize in Tityrus the self-satisfied adherent of the new dictatorial régime ('Amaryllis'), and in Meliboeus the disillusioned man who supported the losing side ('Galatea') but still prefers exile to submission. Some of the exiles are going to Africa (Mexico), some to Scythia (U.S. or U.S.S.R.), while others choose 'the Britons, entirely separate from the rest of the world'. The picture is true for the Italy of 39 B.C., and true no less for the Spain of A.D. 1939. What has enabled it to survive is the 'pastoral convention'. Pastoral is not dead; it may come to life wherever there is a dictator or an inquisition, or a government which revives these methods to keep up its courage. The twenty countries speaking Spanish are certainly not immune. Are there not political implications in *Martín Fierro*, the pastoral epic of Argentina? May we not expect Colombia, with its long tradition of belles-lettres, to reply—and reply pastorally—to the oppressive 'Amaryllis' of the present? Pastoral is not an out-moded form, but a method by which literature may keep itself alive and defend itself from the Philistines, and that was one of the purposes for which it was used by Cervantes.

NOTES

[1] L. Savino, *Di alcuni trattati e trattatisti d'amore del Cinquecento*, in *Studi di letteratura italiana*, 10. (Naples, 1914) and B. Croce, *Trattati d'amore del Cinquecento*, in *Critica*, XL, 233–239.

[2] Margot Arce Blanco, *Garcilaso de la Vega*, in *Revista de Filología Española*, anejo 13. (Madrid, 1930.)

[3] P. Savj Lopez, *Il Cervantes árcade* in *Atti della R. Acc. di Arch.* (Naples, 1906).

[4] F. Egea Abelenda, *Sobre la Galatea de Cervantes*, in *Rev. de Arch. Bibl. y Mus.* n.s. 25 (1921), 554–560.

[5] Vernon Lee, *Studies of the Eighteenth Century in Italy*, 2 ed. (1908), and Giuseppe Toffanin, *L'Arcadia* (Bologna), 1946.

[6] E. J. Dent, Introduction to W. H. and A. F. Hill, *The Violin makers of the Guarneri family*. (1931).

[7] *La Galatea*, Lib. II, *Obras completas de Miguel de Cervantes*, ed. R. Schevill y A. Bonilla (1941), p. 72.

[8] Idem, I., 70.

[9] Idem., II, 134.

[10] Savj Lopez, t.c.

[11] Lib. III, cap. 8.

[12] E. Mele, *Un plagio di Cervantes* and *Il Cervantes traduttore d'un madrigale del Bembo*, in *Giorn. Stor. della Lett. ital.*, XXXIV, 457, 607. It was set to music by Arcadelt, and (in a French translation) by Domenique Phinot. A. Einstein, *The Italian Madrigal* (Princeton, 1949) I, 165, 265.

[13] *Nueva Biblioteca de Autores Españoles*, XXXI, 283 ff., and a separate edition, in 2 vols., ed. E. Juliá Martínez (1950).

[14] Savino, t.c. So also Joaquim Carvalho, *León Hebreo Filósofo* (Coimbra, 1918).
 'Filon e Sofia: amor e a sabidoria, ou melhor, o desejo de saber . . . Sofia é amada não apenas espiritualmente por Filon, e pela ascendência que conquista . . . Filon tendo confessado a Sofia que o conhecê-lhe causa amor e desejo, Sofia responde-lhe que estes dois sentimentos são contrarios.

[15] G. de Lollis, *Cervantes reazionario* (Roma, 1924).

[16] 'Qualche spunto arcadico, e quel sapore campagnolo ringentilito dell'amore e dalla poesia'. Savino, t.c.

[17] *Homenaje a Menéndez Pidal* (1925), 299–321. But see P. Santoro, *Bembo* (1937):
 'E ormai accertato che, tranne una stentata quartina, quei versi non sono suoi. Li copiava de MSS. avuti da Lucrezia o trovati nella biblioteca paterna'.

[18] C. de Lollis, t.c., 19–20.

I

VII

CALDERÓN

THIS essay first appeared, in an earlier and more extended form, in the *Seventeenth Century Studies* presented to Sir Herbert Grierson in 1938, and published by the Clarendon Press. That volume has escaped the Spanish scholars who, since then have expended much thought and labour on the theological ideas which may have been in Calderón's mind; but they might almost be unaware that Calderón's dramatic work was all intended for public performance on a stage before a noisy audience, and not for silent reading in a library.

Alone among students of Calderón, I had the supreme experience, in 1919, of actually seeing an old Spanish mystery play, *El Misterio de Elche*, performed in its traditional, unmodernized, seventeenth-century form; and that experience convinced me that no study of the Spanish drama can be sound, if not based on a thorough knowledge of stage-conditions in which the plays were first performed. It is only then that Calderón's views on theology, Spain, the army or the sense of honour, or his treatment of the relation between appearance and reality, dream and waking, can begin to be appreciated as he intended. Without a sense of the stage, the meaning of Spanish drama is lost.

I

CALDERÓN is the Spanish dramatist whose name is best known to the world at large. Less a poet than Lope de Vega, he owes his distinction, his great contribution to the history of the drama, to his mystery plays, especially those designed for performance in the open air on the feast of Corpus Christi; and the following pages will concentrate mainly on these.

The religious history of Spain, the emphatic quality of the language and the plastic imagination of the Spanish people made Spain peculiarly susceptible to the religious drama; and these conditions were able to take their full effect—long after the public, official religious drama in other countries had come to an end—through the passion for public spectacles of the two Spanish kings whose faces have been made familiar by Velázquez: Philip III and Philip IV. They loved public acts: *autos*. All the world has heard of one kind of public act, through which Spain won an unenviable reputation in the past—the *auto de fe*. There was another kind of *auto*, also a solemn public act, but one which had no victims and no sacrifice beyond a symbolical representation of the Last Supper. That was the *auto sacramental*.

An *auto sacramental* was 'a dramatic composition in one act, allegorical in treatment, and relating as a rule to the Eucharist'. The characteristic feature was the use of allegory. Not all were eucharistic; indeed, in some *autos sacramentales*, the reference to transubstantiation was reduced to a transformation scene at the end; a tableau with the Chalice and Wafer, and the appropriate hymn played on hautboys. The origin of these Eucharistic plays has been looked for in the medieval mysteries. But there is a gap in the pedigree; less is known about the medieval stage in Spain than in France or England. By the sixteenth century, at any rate, two well-marked types of religious plays had survived: the *auto de nacimiento* (nativity play) and the *auto sacramental*. Nativity plays seem to disappear from notice soon after 1600, though a volume called *Navidad y Corpus Christi festejados* (Christmas and Corpus cele-brated) was published in 1664 and included Calderón's *auto* on Beshazzar's Feast. There is sufficient evidence, however, that they went on in a humble way for long after that, out of fashion and altogether too naïve and unsophisticated for an age of baroque art, and the no less baroque theology of the counter-reformation.[1]

Beside the Nativity plays, there were various local mysteries, like the 'Mystery of Elche', a seventeenth-century version of a fourteenth-century Assumption play.[2] It was all sung, like an opera; and ended by a coloured statue of the Virgin Mary being hauled up to heaven, in the dome of the cathedral; while a golden swing (the *araceli*) with the Three Persons of the Trinity sitting in it, came down to meet her, and a crown dangling on a string eventually settled on her head. One of the spectators who had been talking about something else, stopped and gazed upwards: 'By God, that's pretty! *Viva la Santisima Trinidad!*' Then he went on talking. That shows the attitude of the audience, and the attitude of the audience is important. We shall be far from the truth if we imagine Spanish mystery plays being received in a northern attitude of hush and reverence.

2

Nativities and the Mystery of Elche are genuine survivals of medieval religious drama, living on into modern times because people liked them; but in the *autos sacramentales* other influences appeared, and the original conception was profoundly modified. These influences were various and unexpected; there was the growth of coloured statuary, the development of pulpit-eloquence, and the theological ideas of the counter-reformation—all three being characteristic expressions of seventeenth-century Spain.[3]

First, coloured statuary, polychrome sculpture. Though the impulse came originally from Italy, and spread to South Germany where it still survives, it was Spain that became most remarkable for it—Spain and parts of Spanish America: Mexico, Peru, Ecuador; realistic figures, often larger than life, which were put up on the altars in churches, and carried through the streets in processions. There is a museum at Valladolid in Old Castille specially devoted to this form of art; but it is a form of art which critics, examining its products in the cold light of a museum, have judged rather harshly. They forget that these figures were never intended to be museum pieces, but were designed for dramatic purposes, and particularly for a specially dramatic form of lighting: a procession, in the yellow, smoky light of guttering candles, seen through clouds of incense. They are a genuine expression of Spanish religious feeling, alone of their kind, like the Spanish *autos sacramentales*: living pictures in wood or plaster, illustrating Bible narrative and Church tradition, just as the Corpus Christi plays are living and dramatized pictures from the Bible and the Cathechism. The Corpus Christi plays, however, were performed in broad daylight, with living actors, very crudely made up, men and women; for, in Spain, women were allowed on the stage about a hundred years before they were in England.

Other countries drove out their religious plays during the sixteenth century. Spain not only did not drive them out, but made them the expression of reformed catholicism. The ideas peculiar to the theology of the time became prominent, and the *autos* owed their subject-matter to scholastic methods of thought. The *autos sacramentales*, therefore, are not on a level with the medieval mysteries and moralities; they are not remains of these, or survivals, but a new form of dramatic art with an independent cultural basis—that of the counter-reformation; they have as little to do with the mysteries as the later coloured carved figures have with medieval sculpture.

Between the Middle Ages and the counter-reformation lies the Renaissance. In the Spanish drama, the Renaissance is represented by a brief period—from about 1460—in which soldiers, scholars and gentlemen appeared on the stage as shepherds, patriarchs and prophets; while great ladies (like Queen Isabel, before she came to the throne) took the parts of village-maidens or muses. Isabel, in spite of her dropped h's and (so it seemed in Toledo) her rough, north-country accent, appeared as a Muse and recited a piece of verse. The counter-reformation stopped all that. Religion was not a thing to be trifled with; it was a 'business proposition': one had to save one's own soul.

In the formation of *autos sacramentales*, renaissance and baroque both took their share. But in their final form, as Calderón left them, these performances belong entirely to baroque, and are as typical an expression of the counter-reformation as coloured statuary, and the figures which are produced in the Holy Week processions at Seville, when religious brotherhoods and charitable organizations take the statues of their patron saints to pay a nocturnal visit to the cathedral.

The *autos sacramentales* were festival plays, intended for performance on the day of Corpus Christi, which falls at the end of May or the beginning of June. They were given in connexion with a grand procession, in which the Host, under a holy umbrella, protected by a guard of honour with fixed bayonets, and accompanied by all the local dignitaries of Church and State, is solemnly carried round the town. Yet there is evidence, overlooked by most writers on the subject, that some of these festival plays were occasionally performed on other dates and in other circumstances. During the eighteenth century they were performed by students or seminarists at the Escurial, under conditions not far from those of an undergraduate performance to-day. New music was composed, or arranged, for the occasion; and, unlike the music for the original performances, some of it has been preserved. The music must be mentioned, because it played a definite and important part. *Autos sacramentales* were, in fact, a kind of religious or theological opera; and though they were not sung throughout (like the Mystery of Elche), they employed music, dancing and all the arts; while the words (which are all that we have to go upon now) represented little more than the libretto and spoken dialogue of an opera. Calderón, however, was a far better poet than most opera-librettists.

Even more important than words or music was the visual effect;—a predominance of sight over sound and sense, thoroughly in the spirit of the Catholic Church in the seventeenth century. It was as if Catholics in Spain still feared that strange power of belief in things which one could not see, that power shared by all their deadly enemies whom they had destroyed or expelled from their own country: the Muslims, the Jews and the Protestants, for these all worshipped an invisible God, not idols made with hands. So, in a sacred representation like an *auto sacramental*, the stage-pictures were the first consideration; words and music took the second or third place.

The stage-picture, and the manner of presenting it, was peculiar and characteristic. The principle was a bare platform-stage (*tablado*), put up in the open, in a public square; it could be enlarged—and converted into a multiple stage—by the addition of two or more movable stages, constructed on waggons and known as *carros*: 'cars', 'floats'. The nearest that one can get to the *carros* is to think of the triumphal cars of a travelling circus. Some people may still remember what it was like, sixty years ago, to see the procession of Sanger's Circus parading round an English town on the morning of the first performance. There were trumpeters and some sort of band, followed by the heavy, lumbering, gilded cars, decorated in a style which, if debased, was recognizably baroque; with buxom gilded mermaids and caryatides, living nymphs and tight-rope dancers, balanced awkwardly but symmetrically in prominent places; while from a golden chair, at the top of the most decorated waggon of all, a fifteen-stone Britannia precariously ruled the waves with a trident. Then came the elephants, and the cages of lions and tigers and other animals; while near the end of the procession (in about the same position as the Host in a procession in Spain) came Lord John Sanger's chariot, drawn by forty horses four abreast. That is the state of mind—the spectator's state of mind—in which one should approach an *auto* of Calderón.

In the time of Lope de Vega (who died in 1635, when Calderón was thirty-five years old) two simple *carros* were considered to be enough for the performance of an *auto sacramental*. They were placed at the back or sides of a raised platform-stage. These *carros* could open on one side, and the open side formed a small scene which could be closed by a curtain. At the back, they served partly as dressing-rooms, partly to bring the players to the place of perform-ance; but when joined to the platform-stage they provided the scenery, for each *carro* contained one set scene.

Under Philip IV the number of *carros* was increased to four. The author of an *auto* was asked to send in to the local authorities, who had invited him, a memorial of the scenic arrangements he required; and Calderón was no exception to the rule. The Municipal library at Madrid has a collection of these *memorias* written in the poet's own hand, and dated between 1659 and 1681, the year of his death; while at least one earlier *memoria* has been published, dating from 1644. All of them specifically mention four *carros* being required for the performance. The memorial of the scenic arrangements for the *auto* 'The Sacred Parnassus', produced in 1659, required a *carro* with special machinery, so that a mountain could rise from within it during the performance. It is described like this:

The first *carro* for the *auto* entitled 'The Sacred Parnassus' is to be a mountain, painted with trees, fountains and flowers. From this, when the moment comes, will rise, in elevation, another mountain like a pyramid, and on the heights of the peak, a sun among clouds and sunbeams, and within it a Chalice and Wafer. The rest of this second storey will show niches, or breaks in the mountain itself; places to be occupied by ten nymphs, five living and the other five painted and cut out, of the life-size of a woman. . . . All this, as already said, has to be raised to the highest elevation possible, and give one or more turns about the square (when it is first brought on).

The *carros*, before they were opened, sometimes had the form of a globe; and from that, were often referred to as *globos*. We get an idea of what happened from the stage-directions, of which the following are examples:

Hautboys sound and the globe opens, and the PRINCE OF LIGHT is seen in it, in a triumphal car drawn by an angel, an eagle, a lion and an ox, as majestically as possible.

Lo que va del hombre a Dios.

A *carro* opens, and in it is seen, painted, a bookshop; and in the middle a counter, at which PAGANISM (Gentilidad) is seated.

El tesoro escondido.

A trumpet sounds in the first *carro*, which is to be a black ship, with black crew, black pennants at the mainmast, black spars and streamers, painted with serpents for heraldic devices; and pacing the poop, the PRINCE OF DARKNESS AND ENVY, with sashes and feathers and costumes all of black.

El divino Orfeo.

There enters the square a Noah's Ark, imitated as closely as possible and painted on canvas. On reaching the stage, it opens; and in the upper part there is a practicable door with a window in it, from which is a way down on to the stage. By this door, enter NOAH.

La torre de Babilonia.

Some of the most interesting stage-directions in the whole range of the *autos sacramentales* are to be found in 'Thy neighbour as thyself' (*Tu próximo como a tí*), an *auto* written on the parable of the Good Samaritan.

To begin with the thieves. They are SIN, THE WORLD, THE FLESH, and THE DEVIL (*La Culpa, El Mundo, La Lascivia,* and *El Demonio*); and all are dressed as brigands, *de bandolero*, i.e. like the

seventeenth-century highwaymen who infested the roads leading
into Catalonia after the civil war of 1640: a civil war for which
Calderón himself was called up and which (through its horrors)
burnt itself into his memory. Four carros are brought up to the
stage, to be opened one after the other, displaying wild, mountain
scenery. In the upper part of the first carro is SIN, 'dressed as a
brigand, with Gascon cape, hat, belt and pistols'; while the other
thieves appear in turn in the upper parts of their respective carros.
MAN enters, as a traveller, but in smart clothes (*de galán*). He has
a band or ribbon on his hat, adorned with gold and jewels; and
about his neck a chain, from which hangs a heart set with precious
stones. They were given him by a PRIEST and a LEVITE whom he
had met on the road, while an unusually well-dressed SAMARITAN
had given him a ring. MAN has evidently lost his way, or doubts
which path to follow. In one of the two autograph MSS. of the
play Calderón had written: 'Enter as lost . . .'; but he drew a line
through the last two words. Presently someone is heard singing
in the distance. It is GRACE, warning MAN against DESIRE, his own
worst enemy; and while MAN is still pondering the meaning of this
warning, FLESH runs to meet him in the guise of a woman (*La
Lascivia*). She seems to be fleeing from something in terror—or,
as one manuscript has it, she enters half naked, with dishevelled
hair. She faints in his arms; and while he is loosening her laces,
he is overcome by her beauty. To his impatience, the laces seem
ice, and the knot that they make, a fire, a very Calderonian thought.

¡Cómo son hielos los lazos,
y el nudo que dan es fuego!

She soon steals his heart—the heart which he wears (like a
decoration) on his breast—for he is clothed as a gentleman of fashion
of the mid-seventeenth century—and slips away; to return presently
with SIN, the WORLD, and the DEVIL who station themselves
in different parts of the stage, 'with pistols in their hands and masks
on their faces'. Your money or your life!

Rinde la hacienda y la vida.

MAN, as it happens, is not travelling alone. After the departure
of the FLESH, he has fallen in with DESIRE, who has led him into the
trap and now goes over to the other side, drawing another pistol
against him. Then FLESH unmasks and fires. MAN falls, but scrambles
to his feet; the others fire too, 'and MAN (it says) continues falling
and rising again until he is left for dead'.

Then, at the top of the mountain of the first *carro*, a strange piece of theatrical machinery appears; the *devanadera*—literally, the silk-winder or wool-winder—a revolving piece of built-up scenery, with four niches, and practicable descents from the niches to the stage. In the first niche is NIGHT, dressed in black, with stars; and as she descends to the stage she sings verses modelled on the Lamentation of Job, 'Let the day perish wherein I was born'.

> Perezca, Señor, el día
> que al Hombre nacido ve . . .

The LEVITE, who passes by just then, recognizes the quotation, but does nothing to help the wounded MAN. The revolving scene is turned round, and in the second niche is seen the EVENING STAR, 'as St. John the Baptist is painted'; while the PRIEST comments on his song, but once again does nothing for the wounded. The machine is turned again, and in the third niche appears DAWN, in a white tunic and blue cloak; while GRACE comes to meet him from below, and both sing a duet based on the *Magnificat*. Presently the *devandera* is turned once more, and in the fourth niche appears the SUN, 'acted by Him who at first entry played the SAMARITAN'; for the SUN symbolizes God, just as the SAMARITAN symbolizes Jesus Christ.

One should not be too surprised at the pistols. Calderón liked to put his allegorical figures into modern clothes and give them modern weapons. It is startling, however, to find in one *auto* (*El veneno y la triaca*) the figure of Christ—dressed as a merchant—getting the worst of a theological argument with the Devil, and then shooting him with a pistol from behind the scenes.

3

The baroque manner, besides leading to this extraordinary development in religious, festival plays, had also produced an increasing complexity in the form of the speeches. Sermons had been evolving in the same direction. There was a heightening of everything that could affect the senses, particularly the sense of sight; and at the same time great emphasis was laid on the sermon, as a form of art. Speeches in plays, like sermons in church, became show pieces; their form was exactly laid down, their construction followed the laws of rhetoric, while in their verbal expression nothing was omitted which by its force or realism might bring home to the expectant congregation the stench of corruption, the agonies of hell, or the unimagined sensations of the divine presence. Donne and the English preachers of the time are models of restraint compared with their contemporaries in Spain; but Spanish religious oratory (Professor Grierson was the first to point out) left distinct traces on Donne. Donne seems to have been particularly attracted by Spanish literature, both theological and poetical; he was also acquainted with Spanish thought in its most intimate form: popular sayings and proverbs.[4]

The baroque sermon affected the speeches in the later *autos sacramentales*; but (in Calderón, at any rate) the influence was on the rhetorical form rather than the verbal imagery. In verbal expression the *autos sacramentales* stand midway between the baroque sermon and the baroque theatre. Yet it is unlikely that many of the spectators could have heard enough of the words to understand the peculiar beauties of Calderón's language. At the performance of the Mystery of Elche in 1919, I had a privileged position in the Mayor's box or pew, and had read the words and the music beforehand; but the audience kept up such a continuous chatter that I could hardly hear a single word. It is unlikely that Spanish audiences would have been cooler or quieter, in the seventeenth century than in the twentieth. That they enjoyed the verses, however, there can be little doubt, just as the goat-herds enjoyed Don Quixote's discourse on the Golden Age—for the sheer beauty of the sound of the words, without understanding in the least what they meant.

The spectators of an *auto sacramental* were also assisted by the beauty and novelty of the stage-pictures, by the large amount of vocal and instrumental music, and (when they caught the words) by the fact that the authors were apt to repeat themselves, to describe the same thing in the same way, and to use the same kind of imagery year after year—for it should not be forgotten that *autos sacramentales* were festival productions, given only once a year. Calderón himself refers to this fact of annual performance, as an excuse for repetition. In the preface to the only edition of his *autos* published with his consent (that of 1677) he says that readers might find some passages the same; but even in nature some faces were found to be like one another, while it should not be forgotten that performances of this kind were given only once in twelve months. Again, some passages (he thought) might seem insipid; but readers should have regard to the fact that the lines could not be appreciated without the sonorous strains of the music or the magnifi-

ence of the stage setting; while (he went one) 'he that reads must
make in his imagination a composition of the scene, having due
regard to the circumstances'.

The baroque imagery of the verse requires special notice.
Editors and critics have been puzzled by the way Calderón deliberately mixed his metaphors. But Calderón, Professor E. M. Wilson
has shown[5] did not invent this metaphorical procedure; he standard-
ized it. He got it from the poet Góngora, and it has been urged
against him that he reduced the discoveries of Góngora to five or six
set patterns, and exhausted all their possibilities. 'He converted
surprise into a commonplace, form into a stencil, the living classic
into the dead academic', a Spanish critic has remarked.[6] His justifi-
cation must be that he was before all things a dramatist; such flights
of baroque rhetoric would always carry his audience off their feet;
and since his plays were meant to be seen and heard, rather than
read, it was natural that he should sometimes repeat himself if only
for the sake of being intelligible.

4

The developments in staging, and in the use of baroque poetical
imagery for dramatic purposes were not followed by a corresponding
development in ideas. It might almost be said that Calderón was
not interested in ideas, but only in ways of presenting them on the
stage; ideas (at any rate) only attracted him if at the same time they
were dramatic or capable of dramatic treatment by means of his
peculiar methods. This applies also to the controversial, polemical
aspect of Calderón's works, on which Professor Entwistle insisted.[7]

A great deal has been made of his theology; but its importance
may well have been exaggerated. No one sensitive to poetry
would deny the beauty of the theological imagery in Calderón
or of the legal imagery in Shakespeare; but to treat Calderón as a
theologian is like treating Shakespeare as a lawyer. Calderón had
read theology, and knew a good deal; but as a theologian he was
an amateur, while as a man of the theatre, he was a thorough
professional. What he did was to dramatize theological ideas.

In the *autos*, of course, there are many reminiscences of the Bible.
As a priest (for the last thirty years of his life), Calderón had the
right to read the Bible for himself, in the version of the Vulgate;
and his *autos*, taken together, make what is practically a new Spanish
Bible—an illustrated Spanish Bible—in the vernacular. Such a

thing was unknown to Spanish people in general; after the suppression of the reformers and the Spanish vernacular Bible of Cipriano de Valera, the only means by which the Sacred Books could be made intelligible to those who knew no Latin was that provided by the religious poets. But even the works of the religious poets were accessible only to a small number; while the works of the mystics, which have excited so much curiosity since the first world war, were generally neglected for earlier or less alarming works of devotion. It is natural that the poetical books should have attracted him, above all Job and the Psalms; Calderón seems to have had almost as great a veneration for the Psalms as Luther had. It was not only that they spoke to him heart to heart, as they did to the Reformers, and to all oppressed peoples. Calderón was a poet, and felt the Psalms as poetry. Sometimes he translates almost literally; at other times he gives a free rendering and commentary. In almost every *auto* there are quotations, or reminiscences of the poetry of the Psalms; but it is curious and dramatic to find a psalm quoted by the Devil, the Prince of Darkness—*el Príncipe de las tinieblas*, he is magnificently called in Spanish. Yet that is what occurs in the *auto sacramental* founded on the play 'Life's a Dream': 'Lord', the Devil exclaims, 'what is man that thou art mindful of him!' In *El divino Orfeo*, that curious conversion of a pagan myth into a Christian mystery, NATURE, MUSIC and the SEVEN DAYS sing that psalm of which the refrain is 'For his mercy endureth for ever'; while in *El año santo de Roma*, LOVE gives EVERYMAN a prayer-book and tells him to find his place in the Psalms. In *Primero y Segundo Isaac*, DAVID appears in a dream to ELIEZAR, and speaks a Calderonesque version of the opening words of Psalm 80: 'Hear, O thou Shepherd of Israel . . . that sittest upon the cherubim . . . stir up thy strength, and come and help us'. It is curious that angels never appear in the *autos* of Calderón; they are duly admitted and explained by Thomas Aquinas. But the spirits of evil appear, the fallen angels. The greatest of the fallen angels is, of course (we know it from Milton) Satan; and he is always treated very seriously by Calderón, with no suggestion of horns and hooves.

Then there is Death, though he does not appear on Calderón's stage so often as hasty readers have supposed. In 'The great theatre of the Word', Death does not appear at all, though he seems to overshadow every movement of the comedy of life, acted by the seven characters in front of the Producer, who is, in fact, God. On the part of Calderón, this omission was deliberate; and Hofmannsthal, when he introduced the figure of Death into his version for Salzburg and gave him a long and striking part, did not perhaps fully understand Calderón's intention. Hofmannsthal, in fact, in restoring 'The Great Theatre of the World', has treated Calderón rather as the Restoration dramatists treated Shakespeare. The truth is that the figure of Death had become rather old-fashioned for the stage of Calderón's time. He had been a familiar figure ever since the medieval Dance of Death and the time of the great plague; and was still indispensable to the humbler kind of fit-up company; witness the waggon-load of players encountered by Don Quixote, and the comic interlude by Calderón, *La Mojiganga de la muerte*, the Harlequinade of Death, a little piece which shows that Calderón was capable of parodying his own style. In that little play a waggon full of players, ready dressed for the performance of an *auto*, are upset into a ditch. All stagger on to the stage, in their theatrical clothes but in their off-stage personalities, which we have got to know by hearing them talk before the accident; the Devil crossing himself and exclaiming: 'Christ! What a miracle I'm not dead!'; the Angel with a broken head, and a large, property cross, cursing the company for making life so dangerous; the Soul in the arms of the Body, sighing 'Thank you, darling, I feel better now'; while the only one who still remembers to appear, in character, is Death, who enters with an expression of surprise that he should be left until last. Then a tramp, who has been asleep by the side of the road and wakes in terror at seeing so many other-worldly figures, not knowing whether he is dead or dreaming, remarks: 'Well, whoever *didn't* leave Death till last!'

Calderón, however, has occasionally introduced the character of Death into his serious plays and *autos*. In *La cena del rey Baltazar* ('Belshazzar's feast') Death is dressed as a man of fashion, though he is afterwards mistaken for one of the waiters. In *Lo que va del hombre a Dios*, Death and Sin, appear as veiled women, reminding one of Lorca's *Bodas de Sangre* where Death is a beggar-woman, or Cocteau's *Orphée*, in which Death appears as a lady in evening dress and afterwards as a trained nurse. Calderón had anticipated Cocteau by 300 years. In *No hay más fortuna que Dios*, Death appears more conventionally as a skeleton, clutching a sceptre and a spade, after the manner of Shirley:

> And in the dust be equal made
> With the poor crooked scythe and spade.

Shirley was a contemporary of Calderón, and modelled his play
The Opportunity, on a Spanish play by Tirso de Molina; so it is no
surprising to hear Death using almost the same words: *humo*
polvo, *nada* (smoke, dust, nothing) in Calderón and in Shirley
In more than one *auto*, Death enters from a hollow tree where he
has been hidden, and on one occasion he takes the torch from the
hand of Life. But perhaps the most poetical appearance of Death
is that in *La segunda esposa*, where he enters after listening to morta
music, and comes on to the stage humming the tune which the
living have just been singing.

It is true that in the religious plays and *autos* there are passage
which seem a mere parade of scholastic erudition, with an almos
unlimited capacity for performing feats of ingenious deduction from
traditional and accepted premises. Professor Grierson has said
the same of Donne, and compared these 'freakish deductions' with
the 'luminous sense' of Spinoza—a comparison which is equally
justified in the case of Calderón. It was not possible for him, o
for any one else in Spain at that time, to realize how much had been
done 'for the emancipation and healing of the human intellect'
He had to confine himself to the traditional topics of Spanish
devotion.

One of the best known plays of Calderón's is *El mágico prodigios*
('The mighty magician'), scenes from which were translated by
Shelley. It presents the problem of 'Faust', considered from a
Spanish standpoint; but fine though the dramatic situations are, i
seems strangely inadequate for a presentation of doubt. Intending
(like Goethe) to show a spirit which doubts and denies, Calderón
can give only a feeble and ineffective caricature of either doubt o
denial. He knows nothing of contemporary philosophy or freedom
of thought, though he represents his own seventeenth-century
environment with marvellous fidelity. In his own province o
narrow ecclesiasticism, he is unapproachable; but he represents the
arch-angelic insurrection (someone has said) as if it were a contest fo
a professorial chair at Salamanca. His Satan is 'an amiable personage
with no intellectual power or controversial ability worth mention
ing'; and if Cipriano is meant to embody the most extrem
irreligion conceivable, he only shows the feeble powers of a super
ficial mind and remains on the threshold of inquiry, with no con
ception of the insoluble mysteries that lie within. There is little o
Faust's intellectual hunger, or his passionate yearning for omnis
cience, which we find not only in Goethe but in Marlowe.[8]

Other plays which, to a modern mind, seem the quintessence of irony (such as *La devoción de la cruz*) were meant to be taken with complete seriousness. Almost all Calderón's dramas deal with the return and salvation of the soul which has been in danger; but in this play, there seems to be no sin so deadly, but salvation can come of it. It was far from the poet's intention to extenuate crime in the name of the Cross; but that is, in effect, what Calderón has done. The point of the play is that the merit of the Cross is enough to excuse all crimes committed in its name. 'Mark him with a cross, and put him away', says Eusebio, the brigand chief, after one of his men has shot a harmless traveller; and we know that the Recording Angel will take no notice. On this occasion the bullet is stopped by a New Testament in the traveller's breast-pocket; and the brigands are suitably impressed when he walks on to the stage alive and well.

This play, which to some is 'a masterpiece of Christian art', is to others 'a defiance of all reason and common sense'. It seems the *reductio ad absurdum* of Spanish religiosity. How can one reconcile so much piety with so many crimes? There is a big part for Julia; but her recital of the murders she has committed, instead of filling us with disgust and loathing, gives us something of the amused, detached thrill of the modern crime-story. Yet Calderón's attitude was strictly orthodox. He wished to glorify in the criminal the man who, in spite of all the forces tending to drag him down, manages in the end to grasp the reins of his own spiritual destiny. Calderón, in fact, awoke the teaching of the Jesuits to the magic life of the stage.[9]

The scene from the New Testament which made the greatest impression on Calderón was that described in the Acts of the Apostles (viii. 27), in which Philip, going down from Jerusalem to Gaza, met 'a man of Ethiopia, an eunuch, of great authority under Candace, Queen of the Ethiopians', sitting in his chariot and reading the prophet Isaiah. Philip approached and asked the eunuch whether he understood what he was reading; a discussion followed, leading to his conversion and baptism in the first stream the travellers encountered. The essential points of this situation[10] occur in at least five of Calderón's plays: *Los dos amantes del cielo*, *Las cadenas del demonio*, *El Joseph de las mujeres*, *El gran principe de Fez*, and *El mágico prodigioso*. Even the sudden disappearance of the Apostle, caught away by the Spirit of the Lord, is quite in keeping with the magic disappearances which take place in some of the plays just mentioned

—to such an extent was this passage of the Acts before Calderón's mind.

5

The great dramatic idea which haunted Calderón was that of the interaction between appearance and reality, dream and waking. In this he anticipated Pirandello. The thought that all life is only a dream appealed greatly to Calderón's imagination. The chief three examples are *La dama duende*, *La vida es sueño*, and *El gran teatro del mundo*.

La dama duende, 'The goblin lady'[11] is a curious and interesting early play, in which the interaction between imagination and reality is brought out by the idea of fairies. But Calderón treats fairies in a way so foreign to all our ideas—our Shakespearean ideas—as to give us something of a shock. In Spain, fairies are not, and were not in the time of Calderón, a literary convention, as they have become with us. In Spain, fairies were a superstition, and belief in them exposed people to a much-dreaded tribunal—the Inquisition—and 'the secular arm' of the law. Calderón treats fairies in a way which is completely rationalistic. Doña Angela, in the play, finds a secret door opening into the spare room; and on one of the rare occasions when her brother asks a friend to stay with them, she cannot resist the temptation of looking through the guest's luggage, to see whether he has tidy shirts and nice handkerchiefs. Her maid thinks that she may as well act the goblin too, and being a village girl, she changes the money she finds for ashes, in the traditional fairy or goblin manner—the ashes to which 'fairy gold' would turn overnight. Don Manuel the guest, and Cosme his man, are always coming in unexpectedly, and can never imagine why their clothes are in such a mess; and while the man believes firmly in the fairy, the master is convinced that the fairy has flesh and blood. Eventually he catches the fairy (Doña Angela) in the act; while the brother presently finds them together. This is the crucial moment of the play; for brother and sister are in the regular situation of a cloak-and-sword comedy of honour, and the brother will have to kill his sister for being discovered in a compromising situation, or else bring dishonour on the whole family. That, incidentally, is a typical example of the dramatic use of the sense of honour in a Spanish play; and recourse to the 'unwritten law' is only prevented by one of those brilliant theatrical surprises—those *lances de Calderón*—for which Calderón was famous.

La dama duende is something more than a comedy of cloak and sword. The secret door and movable cupboard, by which Doña Angela can get into the spare room 'make it possible to upset the sense of reality of both Don Manuel and his servant. Is the mysterious being a *duende* (as Cosme believes), is she a woman (as Don Manuel eventually discovers), or is she both of these things at the same time, a *dama duende*?'[12] It is the same question as that which is posed by Cervantes in the barber's basin, which for Sancho Panza was only what it seemed, while for Don Quixote it was the helmet of the giant Mambrino. Cervantes makes one see that it was both of these things at the same time (for Don Quixote never ceased to believe it was a helmet); while Calderón, more orthodox and at the same time more rationalistic, convinces his characters, as well as his audience, that the *duende* was really a woman all the time.

La vida es sueño, 'Life's a dream', is a play of the prince who is brought up a prisoner, in ignorance of his true position; but it is also a play of the sleeper who wakes in new and strange surroundings, never knowing when waking ends and dream begins —like Christopher Sly in 'The Taming of the Shrew'. Calderón shows both the dream and the awakening, and Prince Segismundo learns that life is a dream by being put to sleep again, and taken back to the tower. The prince chained in the tower and clothed with rags is, of course, a symbol of unregenerate man, fettered through his senses; and Calderón afterwards converted the play into an *auto*, which reproduces the events, and even some of the lines, of the original play. But it is on another plane, and in another world: the world of the mystery-play. Originally Segismundo had been the symbol of Man; now Man appears on the stage as one of the characters. Instead of the disguised refugee princess Rosaura, there is Grace; instead of Clarín, the comic servant, Will; instead of the earnest tutor, Clotaldo, Reason (or Understanding); instead of a people under a government, the Elements serving Man. Grace invites Man, a prisoner in the mountains, to leave his prison. Man, in the royal palace, makes the Elements serve him. He is misled by Sin and warned by Understanding; but throws him out of the window, as Segismundo does the Second Servant in the play. The torch of Grace is extinguished by Sin, and Man is put back in his tower; but he is saved in the end by the intervention of Divine

K

Wisdom and the Sacraments, and water is brought him in a scallop-shell—a 'scallop-shell of quiet'.

Calderón went even further. As if it were not enough to call life a dream, he would show that it was also a stage: 'The great theatre of the World'. Providence itself should appear as Producer, giving out their parts to men and women; the King, Rich Man, Poor Man, Peasant, Beauty, Prudence and a little Child. Then, after they had played their little play on the stage of the World—the prompter is Grace—the Producer would call them off; and invite all the players on the World's stage to the Lord's Supper, as the manager of a theatre might invite the company to supper after the first performance. As in medieval drama, so in Spanish religious drama of the seventeenth century, there is an extraordinary mixture of sacred and profane, tragedy and comedy, the sublime and the ridiculous. But it does not turn out to be disturbing. For Calderón, Providence is the manager of a theatre, who often directs his theatrical ventures in a way that may seem odd and inscrutable to the players. Calderón knows that the Producer is, after all, a man of the theatre, like Calderón himself.[13]

Calderón once surprised a French abbé by his reluctance to talk; and his reluctance was interpreted as ignorance. He may have had little interest in discussing the rules of French dramatic art or the 'unities'; but his view of life was essentially that of a dramatist. He seems to have been less interested in ideas than in ways of presenting them on the stage; even theological ideas only interested him if they could be dramatized. Yet his allegorical method is of considerable psychological interest. When he staged the struggle that goes on in a man's or a woman's soul between the powers of good and evil, he personified the good and evil impulses, and let the parts be acted by men and women. He was, in a sense, dramatizing psycho-analysis. Conflicts (he would have agreed with Professor C. S. Lewes) are 'not merely an accident of the moral life, they are its essence'. He revived the medieval method of personification and allegory to show how, in a moral conflict, the will is divided and turned against itself. He does not give us character so much as the raw material of character; the passions and emotions which contend for mastery. The unitary soul or personality which interests the novelist is for him merely the arena in which the combatants meet; and the great dramatic achievement of the *autos sacramentales* is that the passions and desires of the psycho-analyst have become the actual dramatis personae in the mystery plays of Calderón.

NOTES

[1] Valdivielso, *Romancero espiritual* (1659) includes a ballad describing a Christmas puppet-show at night: *Ensaladilla del retablo.*

[2] *Music and Letters*, I, no. 2, April 1920, 145–156, and *A Picture of Modern Spain*, 1921 213–230.

[3] Jutta Wille, *Calderons Spiel der Erlösung, eine spanische Bilderbibel des 17. Jahrhunderts.* Munich, 1932.

[4] A portrait of Donne at the age of eighteen shows him dressed as a soldier, with the Spanish motto: *Antes muerto que mudado* (better dead than changed). Twenty-five years later, n a letter to Sir Henry Goodyers, he wrote: 'The Spanish proverb informs me, that he is a ool which cannot make one sonnet, and he is mad which makes two.' This is a reminis-cence of an anecdote in the *Floresta Española* of Melchor de Santa Cruz; see *The Times Literary Supplement*, 12 Sept., 1936, p. 729.

[5] E. M. Wilson, *The Four Elements in the Imagery of Calderón*, in *Modern Languages Review*, XXXI, 1936, 34–47.

[6] Gerardo Diego, *Antología poética en honor de Góngora*, Madrid, 1927.

[7] W. J. Entwistle, *Nueva Revista de Filolgía Hispánica*, II, 1948, 223–238; *Bulletin Hispanique*, L, 1948, 472–482, and LII, 1950, 41–54.

[8] John Owen, *The Five Great Sceptical Dramas of History*, 1896.

[9] Werner Krauss, *Calderon als religiöser Dichter*, in *Der Kunstwart*, XLV, 1931, 490–500.

[10] J. M. de Cossío, *Racionalismo del arte dramático de Calderón*, in *Cruz y Raya*, XXI, Dec. 1934, 37–75.

[11] It was translated for the English stage in 1807 by Lord Holland.

[12] Spitzer, in *Neue Jahrbücher f.Wissenschaft u. Jugendbildung*, VII, 1931, 516–530.

[13] Spitzer, loc. cit.

VIII

BERCEO

I

BERCEO was a poet with books of reference. He was turning into Spanish verse the Latin stories in his books and doing it with a set purpose; he would read his poems to people who could neither read nor write themselves, and for whom Latin had become a mysterious magic language, a sort of hocus pocus rather than a form of speech in which people could communicate with one another. Berceo was using the language in which, he says, a man talks to his neighbour:

> en qual suele el pueblo fablar a su veçino;

and his language, though corrupted by later scribes from different districts, deserves the most careful and detailed study. He went about the country, talking to his neighbours and hearing local traditions. In that he was not unlike the poets and writers of the generation of 1898, who were doing the same thing in the early years of the present century. It was they who discovered Berceo. Azorín imagined him looking out of the window while he was writing, on a spring day. Antonio Machado thought of the monotonous lines of leafless poplars in a Castilian landscape in winter: *monótonas hileras de chopos invernales*—so like Berceo's lines of verse! —with a reminder of the day's work in the brown furrows and a vision of the blue, distant mountains.[1] Manuel Machado would have liked to see Berceo in a carved altarpiece along with Santo Domingo de Silos, a palm-branch in one hand and a glass of good wine in the other. Pérez de Ayala and Enrique de Mesa[2] both felt something fresh in the inspiration of Berceo; but the first modern poet to discover him was Rubén Darío, in his *Prosas profanas* of 1896, and he may well have found him in Menéndez y Pelayo's Anthology which began to be published in 1890.[3] It was not so much his 'ingenuousness' that attracted them: the quality in his poetry which had seemed to a great German scholar, afterwards translated by Unamuno, to be like the magic of a Christmas tree.[4] The poets could not help noticing how accomplished he was

in the difficult technique of his verse, combined with the extreme
bluntness of his language. Something more than a taste for antiques
and the landscape of Castille had made these exceptional minds
detect a new and unaccustomed quality in Berceo. It was not his
scenes or his subjects, but his friendly, confiding manner; the way
he made his subjects come alive and lived in them himself; his
mixture of wide-eyed wonder and rough living expressed with so
much learned artifice. To the generation of 1898, Berceo seemed
different from all other Spanish poets, the embodiment of the
Franciscan ideal of the Spain of that time which descended not only
from the Saint of Assisi but from the example of Don Francisco
Giner.[5]

His period was the end of the twelfth century and the beginning
of the thirteenth. His name was Gonzalo (or Gonçalvo) de Berceo.
Gonçalvo is a Latinized Germanic name, Gundisalvus, brought to
Spain by the Visigoths; Berceo is a village in the Rioja, the wine-
country of north-eastern Castille in the modern province of Logroño.
The poet tells us several times what his name is; he found that it
went well with the kind of verse that he wrote:

> Yo maestro Gonçalvo de Verçeo nomnado[6]

and

> Yo Gonzalo por nomne, clamado de Berceo.[7]

Again, he says that he was at school in the monastery of San
Millán (Aemilianus) and a native of Berceo where San Millán
was born. His signature has been found on various documents
from which it appears that he was born about 1190. The latest signature belongs to the year 1246. He was an ecclesiastic of some sort—
it was difficult for a man who wanted to write to be anything else;
he may have been a monk of San Millán or have belonged to the
clergy of the parish of Berceo. The latter seems more probable.
The title *maestro* (magister) was an ecclesiastical title, not a literary
or educational one; he was *maestro* because he was entitled to hear
confessions.

Berceo wrote about miracles and the lives of saints. He wrote
about them in what one critic was pleased to call a 'dull, jog-trot
metre'—an opinion which must have been the result of sheer bad
reading, and swallowing the unaccented syllables. We should not
condemn Berceo unheard, without reading him aloud. He certainly
wrote about saints and miracles, but no sensitive reader can admit
that either his verse or his treatment is dull. Antonio Machado

said the last word, in his comparison of Berceo's verse with lines
of poplars. The metre is the *cuaderna vía*, the stanza of four verses
of fourteen syllables each, with the same rhyme for all four. The
line has a break in the middle and usually six light stresses, two of
which must fall on the sixth and thirteenth syllables and are accented
with a rise of pitch in the voice. Elision is not allowed. This form
of stanza was known in medieval Latin and old French, and was
called in Spain *mester de clerecía*: the accomplished technique of the
learned clerks, compared with the professional practice of the
wandering minstrels. The former made a point of counting the
syllables; the latter did not. The minstrels had to perform to music
and poetry set to music has never been so exacting in the number of
syllables to the line, for what matter in that case are the stresses
the rhythm of words intended for music is 'irregular' or 'fluctuating'.
One mystically-minded critic has called *cuaderna vía* 'the fourfold
way'; but to translate it like that gives all the wrong associations
The expression *cuaderna vía* may come from boat-building; and a
metaphor from building boats is not inappropriate to the building
of poems, for both have to be seaworthy.

If we open Berceo's most approachable book, the *Milagro*
(miracles), we find the poet addressing us: 'Friends and vassals of
God omnipotent, If you would hear me, of your gentleness' . .

> Amigos e vasallos de Dios omnipotent,
> Si vos me escuchássedes por uestro consiment . . .

Surprising for a 'dull, jog-trot poet'! It sounds superb, and is a
magnificent invitation to an audience. Then he mentions his name
and describes how he went on pilgrimage and found a field: not a
'fieldé full of folk' like Piers Plowman, but a field full of flower
and long grass, a desirable place for a tired man

> logar cobdiçiaduero pora omne cansado.

He describes the scents of the flowers, the streams, the trees and
the fruit; he is careful to say that none of the fruit was overripe or
bitter. He took off some of his clothes, his *ropiella*—his 'airy upper
garments', an English poet (Shirley) would have called them—and
lay down under a tree. Then he noticed how the birds were singing
and that they were singing in tune; like Chaucer, he gives a technical
musical description of exactly how the birds were singing, a description which is perfectly intelligible from what is now known of
medieval music.[9] Then he noticed that both birds and human being
could pick as many flowers as they liked; for every one they took

three or four grew again. The meadow seemed like Paradise itself, Paradise having been originally a word used for a garden—the garden of the King of Persia. The fruit of the trees was sweet and pleasant to the taste, so that 'If Don Adam had eaten of such fruit, he would never have been deceived in such evil manner, nor could Eve and her husband have taken such harm'. 'Gentlemen, friends', he goes on, '*Sennores e amigos*, what we have said is a hard saying; we should like to explain it. Let us take off the peel and come to the pulp.'

2

Before the good man takes off the peel, we can look more closely. We recognize the picture at once. It is a primitive; it has all the characteristics of a painting by one of the early Flemish and Italian masters. It is like the background for a Madonna or a miracle. Berceo's miracles are like the primitive paintings, and his introduction is like the Madonna with her prospect of fields and streams, trees and fruit, and birds singing on the branches. Berceo's inspiration is also like the inspiration of St. Francis of Assisi. Berceo was a contemporary of St. Francis, and had something of the Franciscan passion for birds and flowers. Some writers have imagined that that passion for birds and flowers was all St. Francis's own; that it was he who inspired the whole of primitive painting and a good deal of Renaissance painting as well.[10] That may be an exaggeration, but the feeling and inspiration of the primitives is certainly present in Berceo; we have it, too, in the first and foremost of early English poems, 'Sumer is icumen in'. One has only to think of the words to see how like a primitive painting, how Franciscan—and in a sense, how Bercean—they are.

> Groweth sed and bloweth med,
> And springeth the wudé nu.

They are all primitives, and contemporaries: Francis of Assisi, Gonzalo de Berceo, and the monk of Reading who wrote 'Sumer is icumen in'; primitives with racial and geographical differences. Since they were contemporaries, it would be instructive to consider into what sort of a world they were born. Berceo and the monk of Reading lived in what were peaceful backwaters compared with the surroundings of Francis of Assisi; for the most striking qualities of the age were its turbulence, cruelty and fanaticism. In the year 1200 Latin Christianity had not yet won; it was by no means certain that it would last. In the Mediterranean the language of learning, civilization and commerce was not Latin but Greek. Greek, and then Arabic. Southern Spain, the region most highly developed economically, was still Moslem. Averroes, Maimonides and Ibn Arabi were still alive, though they had all left Spain. The battle of Las Navas de Tolosa, the 'crowning mercy' the Christians called it, was not fought until 1212, when both Berceo and St. Francis were grown up. Córdoba and Seville were not occupied by a catholic king until 1236 and 1248; and after that, the Christian reconquest died down while the Moslem kingdom of Granada survived for another two hundred and fifty years.

The childhood of Berceo, the end of the twelfth century, had seen one of the most ferocious wars in European history: the invasion and annexation of Provence by Northern France, and the destruction of the civilization of the Troubadours on the pretext of a crusade against an unorthodox religious sect, the Albigensians, and indiscriminate massacre on the chance of destroying a few heretics. Berceo was little influenced, if at all, by Provence, though like the poets in Portugal he sometimes used the Provençal device of *leixa-pren* to link his stanzas together.[11] St. Francis's mother had come from Provence, and he had been heard singing to himself songs with Provençal words. He appreciated the minstrels. He wanted to send Brother Pacifico up and down the country singing his *Laudi*, his song in praise of all creatures; and when the moment came for passing round the hat, he and his singers were to say: 'We are minstrels of the Lord, and the reward we ask of you is your repentance.'

A minstrel of the Lord. That was an idea which was firmly fixed in the mind of Berceo also; and it was not merely a metaphor. The man who sang the lives of the saints declared that his matter was better, worthier, than the chanson de gestes. He was scornful of the 'lies' about King Arthur and the Round Table. So the author of a poem on Santa María Egipcíaca (formerly attributed to Berceo) says that his recital will be worth more to the audience than a mere 'fable', a heroic poem:

> Si escucharedes esta palabra
> más vos valdrá que una fabla.

That is not by Berceo. The author of that life of Saint Mary of Egypt was French, translated into Spanish. Berceo was a Castilian, who translated from the Latin; but he still maintained the pose of a

minstrel. At the end of the life of Santo Domingo, he says to the
Saint: 'I call on you for mercy, for I had great desire to be your
minstrel . . . for they say that you are wont to remember your
minstrels'.

> Ca dizen que bien sueles pensar de tus joglares.

The spirit of Berceo cannot be understood unless we think
that the sense of being a minstrel is as genuine in him as it is in St.
Francis.[12] In that age of religious revivalism, the men who sang
about sacred subjects were really known as minstrels of the Lord:
giullari del Signore. St. Francis wished to turn every idea of his time
to the service of his ideal; to convert everything to pious uses,
especially songs and poems. The movement went on for centuries,
both in Italy and Spain; there were *laudi spirituali* set to popular tunes
in Italy, and spiritual parodies of secular poems in Spanish, including
sonnets of Garcilaso de la Vega and madrigals of Gutierre de Cetina.[13]
The Reformers followed suit. French psalm-tunes and Dutch
souterliedekins often originated in taverns; while the most deeply-felt
chorale in Bach's *Matthew Passion* is said to be a parody of an
amorous air from Innsbruck.[14]

Berceo, knowing a little Latin, wished to serve as intermediary
between the learned and the lewd. So he tells us carefully what he
found in the Latin lives of the Saints and other pious documents
preserved in the monasteries. It never occurred to him to parade
his powers of invention; that was not the way for a minstrel of
the Lord to treat pious documents. At one place in the life of Santo
Domingo de Silos, he says quite frankly: 'What happened then,
I do not know; for the book in which I found it failed me. Some
leaves were lost, though not through fault of mine; to write at a
venture would be great folly':

> Perdióse un cuaderno, mas non por culpa mía,
> Escribir a ventura seríe grant folía.[15]

That to invent for oneself, and not copy from a book, would be
great folly is a strange confession from a poet. Again he says: 'There
was a blind man there. Where he came from, the parchment does
not make clear; for the writing was bad, closely-written Latin;
understand it, I could not, by St. Martin!'

> Ca era mala letra, ençerrado latino,
> Entender non lo pudi, por señor San Martino.[16]

It is only by reference to the source, the Latin life of the saint,
that we find the name of the place which Berceo could not read;

it is the familiar Spanish Arabic place-name, Alcázar; *alkozarensi castro*.[17]

The public for which Berceo wrote was the same public for which the minstrels sang. It was not the pilgrims who passed by, not far off, on the road through Santo Domingo de la Calzada to Santiago de Compostela; for the pilgrims were nearly all foreigners, and would not have understood what Berceo was saying, even if they had stopped to listen to him out of curiosity. He wrote for his friends, parishioners, monks, and stray people who came, for one reason or another, to the monasteries of the two chief saints in the district: San Millán and Santo Domingo de Silos.[18] 'I shall write', Berceo says at the beginning of his life of Santo Domingo, 'a poem in Romance, in the language in which a man speaks with his neighbour; for I am not so learned as to do it otherwise in Latin.' And then he adds that characteristic Bercean touch, imitating the style of the minstrels: 'It will well be worth, so I think, a glass of good wine'.

> Bien valdrá, como creo, un vaso de bon vino.[19]

Berceo is always thinking of his audience; and that audience would have included both the few people who were capable of writing their names on legal documents along with Berceo himself, and those who were incapable of writing their names at all.[20] Even kings and queens sometimes preferred to make their marks rather than sign their names. He would write in Romance, so that everyone should understand it

> en romanz, que la pueda saber toda la gent.[21]

Like a minstrel, too, he kept an eye on the audiences so that it should not melt away. 'Friends, if you will wait a moment . . .'

> Amigos, si quisiéssedes un poco atender . . .[22]

'Still, señores, I do not wish to say good-bye; there still remain some little things that I have to say to you':

> Aun non me querría, sennores, espedir;
> Aun fincan cosiellas que vos e de dezir.[23]

'Señores, if you like, while the daylight lasts, of miracles like that I can tell you even more; and if you do not complain, I shall not complain either':

> Sennores, si quisiéssedes mientre dura el día,
> Destos tales miraclos aun más vos dizría;
> Si vos non vos quessássedes, yo non me quessaría.[24]

Berceo did not despise the minstrels; it would be more correct to say that he enriched their repertory. For the poetry in Spanish written by the 'clerks' did not arise in opposition to that of the minstrels; on the contrary, it was derived immediately from minstrel poetry, which was the model for all clerks who began to write poetry in the vulgar tongue. Besides, the minstrels were still the people who spread poetry abroad; and the clerks had to take that fact into consideration when they were writing.[25]

3

Lives of saints and 'miracle-mongering' have been described as a low form of literature; we should not despise it, in the case of Berceo. The lives of San Millán, Santo Domingo and Santa Oria are rewarding. Berceo has unexpected ways of putting things—ways which once seemed to editors and historians of literature to be in very bad taste. There is, for instance, the palsied crone, the woman half paralysed, who is laid before the sepulchre of the saint: Berceo says that she 'lay moaning like a mangy cat':

Yaçié ella ganiendo como gato sarnoso.[26]

Again, when Santo Domingo is dying in agony, the poet says that he positively enjoyed his pain, 'as if he were eating a fat trout'. Berceo must have been something of a fisherman, for he tells us that the saint 'knew how to cast a hook at the devil'.

Though the lives of the saints by Berceo provide occasional felicities, the Miracles are worth more attention. They should not be read like the short stories of Anatole France, though sometimes they are on much the same subject. Berceo's miracles are often good stories, specimens of the art of story-telling, rather than hagiography or miracle-mongering. One of the best is the tale of Teófilo, once told by Hrostwitha. Teófilo had been chaplain to a bishop; and when the bishop died, everyone was in favour of Teófilo being appointed bishop himself. He, however, was a holy and humble man of heart, contented with his state of life, and declined the honour. Another bishop was appointed and with him he brought another chaplain. Then for the first time Teófilo regretted his decision. He found himself a person of no importance, kept in ignorance of all the intrigues of the diocese which in former times he had found so interesting. He resented it, and moped; and the devil, who is never far off on those occasions, met Teófilo at the cross-roads and asked whether he could be of any assistance.

Teófilo sold his soul to the devil, on condition that he might once more be an important person in the bishop's palace. He was restored to favour, and made even more important than before . . . until remorse came, and repentance. But it was all put right by the Virgin Mary, and hushed up. Teófilo saved both his soul and his reputation.

The meeting with the devil had been arranged by a learned Jew who, Berceo says

> con la hueste antigua avie su cofradia.

What was the *hueste antigua*? We find it to be the origin of the modern word *estantigua*; an apparition, phantom, goblin, or a person who looks as if he had seen one. It is a contraction of HOSTIS ANTIQUA, the ancient host: a procession of phantoms, *the* procession of phantoms, the ancient host of the dead.

The Jew took Teófilo at dead of night to a place where four roads met, the traditional place for holding converse with the devil. In Spanish folklore, Baroja points out in an essay,[27] the procession of souls in torment was always led by one of the devils. In Berceo's version, the Jew took Teófilo by the hand, telling him, whatever he did, not to make the sign of the Cross. The procession passed with lighted candles. He was led into a tent where the *sennor* was sitting. The *sennor* was the devil himself, who received him with great honour, while the other princes of evil sat round them.

> Recibiolo el rei asaz a grand onor.
> Si fizieron los prinçipes quel sedien derredor.

That seems to be the oldest description of the phantom army in Spanish literature. In the Poem of Fernán González, more than a century later, it is mentioned almost as a joke, something so well known that it can be treated with familiarity or contempt. The retainers of Count Fernán González complain of their wandering life; they are always on the move, they say, like the *hueste antigua*. We find it, too, in a Scottish Border Ballad, but taken seriously in the style of Berceo—the Ballad of Tam Lin; and the phantom host is described with unusual vividness because it is not seen but heard. There are no candles or torches, but we know that the host is riding by because we hear the bridles ring.

> About the dead hour o' the night
> She heard the bridles ring:
> And Janet was as glad at that
> As any earthly thing . . .

> And first gaed by the black, black steed,
>   And syne gaed by the brown;
> But fast she gript the milk-white steed
>   And pu'd the rider down.

> She's pu'd him frae the milk-white steed
>   An' loot the bridle fa',
> And up there rase an eldritch cry
>   'True Tam Lin, he's awa'.'

Tam Lin is changed by the fairies into various symbolical forms while Janet holds him: into an 'aske' (newt), a snake, a deer, and a hot iron at the fire; and then

> They shaped him in her arms at last
>   A mother-naked man;
> She cast her mantle over him,
>   And sae her love she wan.

The *hueste antigua*, then, was a procession of apparitions or souls. We remember that procession which Don Quixote and Sancho once saw: a long procession, at night, of people carrying lighted torches. They turned out to be a great funeral procession carrying the body of a dead man to the place where he was to be buried, a long way off; but the fright of Sancho Panza and the courage of Don Quixote came from the fact that both thought the procession could be nothing else than the *hueste antigua*.

The miracle of Teófilo is typical of the 'scenes of clerical life' which Berceo depicts. But he can give us other scenes too. We see the Blessed Virgin Mary accompanied by two angels with a bright light, coming down to perform an operation on an abbess, the night before an episcopal visitation. We hear the startling language used by thirteenth-century bishops when full of righteous wrath. 'Never, from a priest, have I heard such a thing!' he said. 'Tell that son of a —— to come to me!' The ignorant priest was dismissed from his chaplaincy; but the B.V.M. appeared to the bishop, in a dream. 'She told him strong things, an angry little sermon; she laid bare all her heart to him.' She talked as Queen Victoria might have talked, or would have liked to talk, to a bishop who had annoyed her.

The fifteenth miracle is related to a well-known medieval story: that of the man who, in earnest or in jest, became betrothed to Venus, and then was prevented ever after from consummating an earthly marriage. He went to bathe, in a bathing pool like the one in my own college, with busts or statues round it. He undressed and slipped his engagement ring on the finger of a statue of Venus. When he came out of the water, he found that the finger of the statue had closed on the ring. That, more or less, is what happens in the story by Prosper Mérimée, and in the poem by William Morris, 'The Ring given to Venus'. But in the Middle Ages, statues of Venus sometimes underwent a curious transformation. They were converted to Christianity, decently draped and put up in churches; there are several well-authenticated cases, in Italy and elsewhere, in which a Graeco-Roman statue of Venus has become a venerated and wonder-working image of the Virgin Mary. So the story of the ring came to be applied to the Virgin Mary instead of Venus, and that is what has been done by Berceo.

He has simplified the story and left out the ring; but the story is essentially the same. The man is a canon, an only son, who is persuaded for family reasons to leave the Church and marry. When the wedding-day came, he went with his relations and friends to fetch the bride home; but he found that he could not meditate on the Blessed Virgin as he used to do. And as he was ruminating on these things, they passed a church. He left the others at the gate, and went in to say his prayers. The Virgin, *La Gloriosa*, came to him in a fury.

Don fol, malastrugado, torpe e enloquido . . .

'Sir Fool, unfortunate, madman, idiot! Where are you going? Into what have you fallen? You must be bewitched, as if you had drunk poison; or you have been touched by the rod of St. Martin and gone out of your mind. Was it not enough that you were well married to me: *bien casado conmigo*? I loved you dearly as a good friend; but you must needs go looking for better wheaten bread. For all that, you are not worth the worth of a fig.' (Here she must have made the sign with her fingers and thumb which Santa Teresa was taught by her confessor to make at the devil.) 'If you will listen to me and believe what I say, you will not give up your former life. You will not leave me, to take up with another woman. If you do, you will have a pretty bundle of wood to carry on your back!' That was what the statue of the Virgin Mary said to the bridegroom while he was praying in the church. He went out, admonished; they all complained that he had kept them waiting. The marriage was celebrated; but the bridegroom was snatched away from the arms of the bride, and none ever knew what had happened to him. But *La Gloriosa* knew, and kept him well hidden.

This is translated straight from Berceo's fifteenth miracle: a pagan story, thinly Christianized. A Graeco-Roman statue of Venus converted into a little dark Spanish Madonna, who came down from her altar in a rage, using the most abusive language, because one of her worshippers had gone after a fairer woman! Notice the language she uses: the language of a Castilian countrywoman of those days. Notice the phrase *mejor pan de trigo*, 'better wheaten bread', that is to say, whiter bread, implying that the other woman was fairer than she was. In Spain, all the oldest and most miraculous images of the Virgin Mary—Guadalupe, Montserrat, El Pilar, and the rest of them—are all very dark, *muy morena* or *trigueña*, swarthy or almost black. The carving is attributed to St. Luke, and the wood has turned black through time and their being buried in the earth during the Moorish occupation.

4

The sources of Berceo's lives are the obvious ones. The saints are often local saints, and there was generally a Latin biography by some devoted disciple who had lived with the holy man, like Grimaldo who wrote the life of Santo Domingo de Silos. The life of San Millán was written by San Braulio, Bishop of Saragossa in the seventh century; but we miss in his Latin the quick eye for detail which we find in Berceo's Castilian: in the passage, for instance, describing how the saint began life as a shepherd boy and took a musical instrument with him.[28] In the life of the holy virgin Santa Oria, the biographer was her confessor. But as to Berceo's Miracles, what was the origin of them? It used to be held that Berceo drew all his miracles from France; their origin must be the collection of *Miracles de la Sainte Vierge* by Gautier de Coincy, a contemporary of Berceo's who died in 1236. Berceo was merely translating and imitating the French author. It was not so simple, however. When the two versions were compared, there were seven miracles in Berceo which could not be found in the French; and it was noticed that though Berceo had not the literary skill or tradition of Gautier de Coincy, he survived comparison with him through his power to select significant incidents and his eminently Castilian gift of realistic vision. For these and other reasons it was thought likely that both Berceo and Gautier de Coincy had derived their miracles from some earlier collection in Latin. Then the identical collection, or one very near the collection which Berceo himself may have used, was discovered in the Royal Library at Copenhagen.[29] It is a Latin manuscript in which twenty-four out of Berceo's twenty-five Miracles are to be found, and they are in the same order that Berceo gives them.

Berceo's Life of Santa Oria is interesting for other reasons: it leads to the question of allegory. The *Vida de Santa Oria* is a series of visions experienced by the saint and her mother; and the chief of them, the centre of the whole composition, is Oria's dream of how she went up to heaven and saw a throne prepared for her. There was a long flight of steps, a mysterious tree, and a still more mysterious figure, called Voxmea, standing beside the empty chair which was waiting for Oria.

There is another mysterious journey in the life of Santo Domingo de Silos. Domingo comes to a gloomy place where there are two streams, one white and the other crimson. He crosses a narrow bridge of glass, a very dangerous crossing, and is met on the other side by heavenly messengers with crowns.

We are in the world of medieval allegory. Berceo is before Dante—he died before Dante was born—yet visions and allegories were the fashion with religious writers in all countries, and not only countries which were Christian. Moslem countries had their allegorical writings too; one Moslem Spanish writer, Ibn Arabí of Murcia, a contemporary of Berceo, foresaw Dante's Hell, purgatory and paradise so clearly that it is impossible to believe that some knowledge of Moslem thought had not filtered through to Dante at the time of his vision in 1300.[30]

In the use of allegory by Berceo we find three different stages.[31] The three stages are interesting and important—interesting because they show things which were at the back of the medieval Spanish mind, and important because they were also stages in the development of literary technique. After all, Berceo was a writer; and it is worth while to study his art of writing, the way he arranged his ideas and conveyed them to his audience. In the use of allegory by Berceo we find three different stages, both of allegory and of the art of writing.

The first stage is represented by the Miracles. At the beginning, in the introduction, there is the description of the garden, with all the flowers and birds—the description which reminded us of pictures by the primitive painters: everything clear and bright and exact, 'a lasting spring'. This, however, is a medieval garden, which means to say that it is an allegory; and in this instance everything in the garden is explained as an attribute of the Virgin Mary. There the allegory ends. It is not connected directly with the rest of the book, which tells the stories of twenty-five of the Madonna's miracles. The allegory is not part of the main composition of the picture; it is the frame, the setting.

The second stage in the development of allegory we find in the life of Santo Domingo: the vision of the three crowns brought by heavenly messengers. The saint has just crossed the dreadful bridge; and there, on the other side, he finds angels waiting for him with golden crowns. The crowns, of course, have their meanings: one is for the pious observation of monastic vows, one for devotion to the Madonna, and the third for having refounded the monastery. The allegory is kept up to the end; its explanation is all part of the general composition, and its presentation reminds one of a mystery play.

The third stage in the use of allegory we find in the life of Santa Oria; the principal interest lies in the vision itself, and there is no prosaic explanation to disturb it. It holds one's attention like the account of a journey and the things which were seen on the way. It looks forward to the great Spanish literature of travel and discovery.

5

There is one other poem by Berceo which is worthy of notice because it includes that wonderful early Spanish lyric printed as No. 2 in *The Oxford Book of Spanish Verse*, the 'Song of the Sentries' —a song of incoherent words, mostly nonsense, with a refrain repeated after every line, *Eya velar*.[32] The poem of Berceo from which this lyric is taken is entitled *El duelo que fizo la Virgen María* (the lament which the Virgin Mary made); it is the story of the Passion told as a Castilian mother in the early thirteenth century would have told it of her own son. She says that she was 'toasted' and 'grilled' by the pain of it:

> Ca yo fui biscocha, et fui bisassada.

They cared nothing for her cries, not 'three oak-apples':

> Ellos por las mis voces tres agallas non daban;

but gave Him to the 'Moors' to be crucified:

> Diéronlo a los moros que le fuesen colgar.

L

Yet she knew that, against God, men's wits were weak and short;
'not worth a pot with a hole in it':

> El seso de los omes flaco es e menguado,
> Non vale contra Dios un tiesto forado.

The questioner is 'Sant Bernalt', St. Bernard of Clairvaux, whose
tract *De Planctu Beatae Mariae Virginis* is usually given for the source
of Berceo's poem. Closer, however, is the *Meditatio in passionem et
resurrectionem Domini*.[33] Yet neither of these is very close. The idea
is vaguely there, but not Berceo's treatment of it; and we find in
St. Bernard no trace of the Song of the Sentries.

The original of *Eya velar* is to be found elsewhere. That phrase,
the same as it is in Berceo's poem, was used by sentries on the walls
of Modena, in Italy, about the year 900. There is a medieval Latin
poem, urging the sentries not to go to sleep:

> Resultet echo 'Comes, eja vigila',
> Per muros 'Eja' dicat echo 'vigila'.[34]
> 'May the echo resound: "Comrade, heigh, there! Look out!"
> On the walls may the echo say: "Heigh, there! Look out".'

This medieval Latin poem of the sentries on the walls of Modena
helps us to the refrain *Eya velar*; and it helps us to the poetical idea,
the *evocación* of sentries calling to one another in the dark. The
evocation is there, too, in the name of the town of Tetuán, in Spanish
Morocco, which is said to be derived from a Berber word used by
sentries, calling to one another at night to keep their eyes open
Tittâwîn! Tittâwîn!—a dual form—'Your two eyes!' or 'Both your
eyes!'

The shout of the watchman on the walls is found in other places in
Spanish literature, besides Berceo. It comes into one of the old
ballads about Peter the Cruel:

> Velá, velá, veladores, así mala rabia os mate.

There are various references to it in Lope de Vega.[35]

The suggestion of watching by a tomb does not come only from
the story of the Crucifixion. It is a piece of folklore, found in many
races, and particularly in Semitic races. The watch of three nights,
by the tomb or dead body occurs also in European folktales, e.g.
The Grave Mound in Grimm. In this story it is the devil who attempts
to carry away the dead man. The removal of the corpse from the
grave is considered to be a disaster, because the spirit which once
inhabited that desecrated body can henceforth have no rest.[36]

The origin of the song of the sentries is, of course, that passage in the Gospels where the Jews go to Pilate and ask for a guard to watch the tomb of Christ so that the disciples shall not come and take the body away. Pilate replies, 'Ye have a watch; see ye to that'. The apocryphal gospel of St. Peter,[37] however, provides vivid poetical touches not found in the synoptic gospels, e.g. when on Good Friday there was darkness over all the earth, 'many went about with lamps, supposing that it was night; and some fell'—a touch like those with which Berceo gave new life to his own stories. Peter gives a fuller account of the Jews asking for sentries than the four Evangelists do. There was Petronius, the centurion—Berceo calls him *Centurio, un noble caballero*—and at least four Roman soldiers. Some Jewish elders and scribes came with them, they sealed up the tomb and went away.

Berceo makes the Virgin Mary describe how the Jews came to Pilate to ask for a guard. They were afraid of being made ridiculous. 'His disciples will laugh at us. They will mock us and make songs about us.' Pilate refused. 'You have sentries enough and strong men of your own. Guard the sepulchre yourselves; make your own songs. Surround the tomb with good sentries, men who will neither drink, nor sleep at their posts.' So they returned to the tomb in their coats of mail, 'saying many foul, hostile things with their lips and singing songs not worth three figs; playing on musical instruments: lutes, viols and fiddles. The ruffians sang ribald songs, which were bitter for his mother and hard to bear. "Alhama, Sanhedrin! Let's watch and be wise, If not, they'll laugh at us and mock us".'

Then Berco's song begins:

Eya velar, eya velar, eya velar!

Heigh there, awake! Keep a look-out! The words which follow are more or less nonsense words, but the imagination of Berceo has caught the whole scene: the shadowy forms with spears round a grave, calling to one another; and the answer coming from a short distance away out of the darkness. One man singing his ribald, doggerel verses; and another answering him after every line with *Eya, velar.* The effect is magical, and Berceo is a poet because he enables us to see it and hear it; because he convinces us that, whether he had imagined it or had seen it acted in church, it can only have happened in that way.

NOTES

[1] Azorín, *Al margen de los clásicos*. (Residencia de Estudiantes, Madrid, 1915); Antonio Machado, *Mis poetas*, in *Obras*, No. 60. (Ed. Séneca, Mexico, 1940).

[2] Manuel Machado, *Glosa* in *Museo*; Pérez de Ayala, *Con sayal de amaguras*, in *La paz del sendero*; Enrique de Mesa, *El bon vino*, in *Cancionero castellano*.

[3] Rubén Darío, *A Maestre Gonzalo de Berceo*, in *Prosas profanas*. Rafael Ferreres, *Un aspecto de la crítica literaria de la llamada generación de* 98. (Castellón de la Plana, 1950), agrees that Rubén Darío was a reader of Menéndez y Pelayo. He quotes Azorín that the writers of 98 went to Berceo *como reacción contra la ampulosidad en literatura*. To the emphasis and artificiality of Castelar, Núñez de Arce and Echegaray, they opposed the simplicity and spontaneity of the primitives; they claimed to have found in Bercco and the Archpriest of Hita a new poetry for modern times.

[4] Ferdinand Wolf, *Studien zur Geschichte der spanischen und portugiesischen Nationalliteratur*. (Berlin, 1859); translated by Unamuno, (Madrid, 1895).

[5] Américo Castro, *The Structure of Spanish History* (Princeton and Oxford, 1954) published —like E. R. Curtius' *Europäische Literatur und lateinische Mittelalter* (Bern, 1948), the only other important modern contribution to Berceo—after the present chapter was written, has suggested that the nearest things to Berceo's lives and miracles are the lives of the holy men of Moslem Spain, published by Miguel Asin Palacios, *Vidas de santones andaluces* (Madrid-Granada, 1933).

[6] *Milagros*, 2.

[7] *Santo Domingo*, 767. The best study of Berceo's prosody, and the manner of reading his verse (especially the diphthongs) is that of F. Hanssen, *Anales de la Universidad de Chile*, Feb. 1897.

[8] P. Henríquez Ureña, *La versificación irregular en la poesía castellana*, 2 ed. (Madrid: Centro de Estudios Históricos, 1933).

[9] F. Pedrell, *Organografía musical antigua española*. (Barcelona, 1901), 121–122.

[10] Henry Thode, *Franz von Assisi und die Anfänge der Renaissance in Italien*. (Vienna, Phaidon; 4 ed. 1934). Analogous conclusions are reached by Johan Nordström, *Moyen âge et Renaissance* (French translation, Paris, 1933), and J. CorteSão, in *Historia de América*, III, 508–513 (Buenos Aires, 1947).

[11] Especially in the *Duelo*, cf. 46–47, 49–50, 71–72, 79–80, 99–100, 109–110, 139–140, 155–156.

[12] R. Menéndez Pidal, *Poesía juglaresca y juglares*. (Madrid: Centro de Estudios Históricos, 1924).

[13] Both were set to music by Francisco Guerrero, *Canciones y villanescas espirituales* (Venice, 1589).

[14] *Innsbruck muss ich dich lassen* became *O Welt, muss ich dich lassen*; in English, 'O Sacred Head, surrounded . . .'

[15] *Santo Domingo*, 751.

[16] Idem, 609.

[17] Amador de los Rios, *Historia crítica de la literatura española*, III, 250. (Madrid, 1862). *Alkozarensi castro* is, strictly speaking, tautological, since the Arabic al-quaṣr is itself derived from the Latin CASTRUM.

[18] G. Cirot, *L'expression dans Gonzalo de Berceo*. Revista de Filología Española, IX, 1922, 154–170.

[19] *Santo Domingo*, 2.

[20] Cirot, loc. cit.

[21] *Martirio de San Lorenzo*, 1.

[22] Milagros: *La deuda pagada*, 1.

[23] *Vida de Santa Oria*, 185. *Oria* is the Latin AUREA.

[24] Milagros: *El náufrago salvado*, 1.

[25] Menéndez Pidal, loc. cit. 352.

[26] *Santo Domingo*, 586.

[27] *Ahora*, Jan., 27, 1935. Virgil also, on one occasion, 'heard the bridles ring', *Georg.* III, 84.

[28] *Sancti Braulionis Caesaraugustani Episcopi Vita Sancti Emiliani*. Ed. crítica por Luis Vázquez de Parga. (Madrid, 1943).

[29] Richard Becker, *Gonzalo de Berceos Milagros und ihre Grundlagen* (Strassburg, 1910).

[30] See Miguel Asín Palacios, *La escatología musulmana de la Divina Comedia* (1919) and the controversy it aroused.

[31] C. R. Post, *Medieval Spanish allegory* (Harvard University Press, 1915).

[32] There has been some discussion on the proper order of the stanzas. See *Nueva Revista de Filología Hispánica*, IV, 1950, p. 50, and V, 1951, p. 226. The most convincing arrangement is that adapted by Dr. F. Brittain in *The Medieval Latin and Romance Lyric* (Cambridge, 1937 and 1951).

[33] Migne, *Patrologia Latina*, especially vol. 184, col. 758.

[34] *O tu, qui servas armis ista moenia*. *Oxford Book of Medieval Latin Verse*, No. 36; Brittain, t.c., pp. 86–87.

[35] *Las almenas de Toro, El nacimiento de Cristo*, and *La Dorotea*. See Menéndez Pidal, *La primitiva poesía lírica española*, (1919) reprinted in *Estudios literarios*.

[36] E. S. Stevens, *Folk-Tales from Iraq* (1923), 302.

[37] Montague Rhodes James, *The Apocryphal New Testament* (1924). See also G. Guerrieri Crocetti, *Gonzalo de Berceo*. (Brescia, 1947).

IX

MEDIEVAL LYRICS

I

NONE of the older Spanish lyrics are more memorable than the *serranillas* or *pastorelas*. They are found, too, in Portuguese, to say nothing of Old French, Provençal and Italian; but the subject is always the same: the meeting of a cavalier and a mountain-girl or shepherdess, familiar in English folk-song:

> As I walked out one May morning,
> One May morning so early,
> I overtook a fair pretty maid
> Just as the sun was rising.
>
> Her shoes were black, her stockings white,
> Her buckles shone like silver.
> She had a dark and rolling eye,
> And her hair hung down her shoulder.
>
> 'How old are you, my fair pretty maid?
> How old are you, my honey?'
> She answered me right cheerfully:
> 'I'm seventeen come Sunday'.

That was as it might be in seventeenth- or eighteenth-century England; but in the Middle Ages the maid with the dark and rolling eye might be a demon, one of those spirits known to monastic scribes (and also to monastic pharisees) and called *silvaticae*: things which personified the forces of nature and fertility and came out to tempt wayfarers with their bare feet.

In Germany, the meeting was generally with a goose girl, like those in *Grimm's Fairy Tales*; but in Spain (with France, Portugal, Italy and above all Provence) the story was told lyrically, in stanzas, and generally with a refrain. There are famous Spanish examples, particularly by the fifteenth-century Marqués de Santillana and the fourteenth-century Arcipreste de Hita. With the former, the thing is treated exquisitely and not without a touch of *donjuanismo*; the noble marquess was clearly a connoisseur of *serranas*. 'In all my born days—I never saw milkmaid—like her of this morning':

> Desque nací
> non ví tal serrana
> como esta mañana.[1]

158

Then he trots back in mind to the scene in which he saw her, with the names of the places he passed on the way. The early fruit gave him an appetite:

> Allá en la vegüela
> a Mata el Espino,
> en esse camino
> que va a Loçoyuela,
> de guisa la ví
> que me fizo gana
> la fructa temprana.

Nothing came of it, and another day he met another *serrana*, while he rode half asleep in a wild part of the country where he had lost the way. Once more, the place-names are part of the evocation:

> Faziendo la vía
> del Calatraveño
> A Sancta María
> vencido del sueño
> por tierra fragosa
> perdí la carrera,
> do ví la vaquera
> de la Finojosa.[2]

She said no, too. But then there was the *moçuela de Bores* . . .

> e nos avenimos.
> E fueron las flores
> de cabe Espinama
> los encubridores.[3]

'And so we agreed—and there were the flowers—all round Espinama—to shield us from sight.'

These are the rhymes of a man on horseback, who gallops away— we hear the horse's hooves in the verse—when once the adventure is over. It was always fine weather when the noble marquess saw his *serranas*; but with the archpriest it was usually raining or snowing, and the verse is the laboured tread of a man not riding but toiling up the mountain paths on foot. Once more, the geography is exact; it is possible to mark the archpriest's progress on a map.[4]

> Cerca la Tablada
> la sierra passada,
> falléme con Aldara
> a la madrugada.

Coming down from the pass, the Puerto de Guadarrama, and running to keep warm in the cold mist and frost, he was stopped by a *serrana*; but she was as ugly as sin. The archpriest knew from his calling that sin, of course, is always ugly; moreover, he wished to parody the style of the troubadors and cavaliers and tell us what the *serrana* was really like. But the adventure ended in the usual way.

The theme was eventually taken up by the ballad-singers. There is a ballad of a *serrana* meeting a traveller on the road to Ciudad Real in La Mancha. In the poem it is called Villa Real, and that helps to date it; for Villa Real changed its name to Ciudad Real in 1420. The poem is a lyric turning into a ballad; the metre, like the arch-priest's, shows the heavy-footed weariness of a man who has lost the way.

> Yo me iba, mi madre,
> a Villa Reale;
> errara yo el camino
> en fuerte lugare.[5]

We notice that many words at the end of the lines—*reale, lugare*, and others—have a final e; the *e paragógica* of Spanish prosody. This is due to the tune—one of the most beautiful of all old Spanish tunes—which make a final syllable essential to the song.[6]

The poem is about a man telling his mother of the curious adventure which befell him on the road to Ciudad Real. He lost his way in a wild part of the country, and went on for seven days without eating bread. Somewhere between two wayside inns, still marked on a seventeenth-century map and one of them having the Arabic name Darazutane,[7] he lifted up his eyes to the east and saw a hut; smoke was coming from it. He dug his heels into the mule and went in that direction; sheep-dogs came out to bark at him. He saw a *serrana* who looked a fine, upstanding young woman; and she said: 'Dismount, pretty gentleman, don't be shy! My father and mother have gone to the village, and my young man has gone to buy bread and won't be back to-night.'

What this theme became eventually we see in the ballad of *La Serrana de la Vera*.[8] The *serrana* has been abandoned by her lover, and, rather in the style of the archpriest's *serranas*, entices men into her hut to murder them next morning. One day, however, a man comes who is more alert than most. He notices a pile of skulls in a corner, and carefully leaves the door ajar when told by the *serrana* to shut and bolt it. After supper, they both make music; but the man sings such an interminable ballad that the *serrana* goes to sleep, only waking to find that her prey has escaped.

This ballad was made into a play by Lope de Vega, and also into a mystery-play by him—an auto *sacramental*—and again into another play by Vélez de Guevara. In this play, like so many in the golden age of Spanish literature, the chief characters are given names of important people; the man going to Ciudad Real becomes the Master of the Order of Santiago, and in the third act the son goes out to fight the Moors. In the mystery-play, on the contrary, the characters are all abstractions: Man is going towards the heavenly city, and the *serrana* is Lasciviousness enticing him out of the direct road. While Man is in her hut he is set upon by bandits: Forgetfulness, the World and Deception, who are all in league with the *serrana*. But it all ends happily. Some shepherds pass by and get him away from the bandits, and one of them turns out to be the Good Shepherd Himself.

2

Though ballads became the dominant form of traditional Spanish poetry—the form carried to Morocco and the Near East by the exiled Spanish Jews, and to Spanish-speaking America by the *conquistadores* and colonists—in Spain and Portugal the lyrics went on all the time; the substance changed but the form survived.

In Spain the Middle Ages have never really come to an end. At the beginning of the sixteenth century, Spaniards did not turn their backs on the Middle Ages, like the Italians, the French, and the Portuguese; Spanish writers, poets and thinkers, without shutting themselves off from the new influences of the moment, still went on in the medieval tradition. That is one of the most original things about Spain and Spanish literature: its great secret, the key to its strength, the explanation of its restlessness. There is, Dámaso Alonso says, a vein of medievalism running through all Spanish things. It comes out strongly in Spanish literature; in the ballads, the popular lyrics and the proverbs. The 'vein' might almost be called a stream. It rises in the Middle Ages and flows strongly in the sixteenth century. This is the age of the great collections of ballads (*Romanceros*) and the various collections of cultivated lyrics (*Cancioneros*). It is also the age of the great collections of popular and traditional lyrics, and in this sense plays became collections of lyrics too, especially the plays of Gil Vicente and Lope de Vega, and so did the lyrical poems of Camões and Góngora.

Lope de Vega is the most conspicuous example; but how far were these poems really by Lope? Perhaps it is better, and safer, to follow Dámaso Alonso, and call them *poesía de tipo tradicional*. The sixteenth century, at any rate, was the century in which ballads and poetry of a traditional type were great and inspiring influences on everyone who wrote or read or listened to poetry.

Traditional lyrics include the short, popular poems which Gil Vicente and Lope de Vega included in their plays, and which Camões and Góngora used for the starting-points of original poems; the poetry which these poets would have heard people singing up and down the country. These songs are of two kinds; there are two different principles which, however, may sometimes be combined in the same poem. There is the form with a refrain at the beginning, and repeated wholly or in part, with the same rhyme, after each stanza, and the form arranged in parallel stanzas ending in the same line. These two forms have various names: the popular lyric with a refrain (*estribillo*) at the beginning is generally known as a *villancico*, while the lyric in parallel stanzas was called by Aubrey Bell a *cossante*.

The word *villancico* has a long history in Spanish poetry and Spanish music. It has come, now, to mean something like a Christmas carol, but originally it was a short poem sung by country people—by *villanos*, 'villeins' (cf. French *villanelle* and Italian *villanesca*)—and with the refrain at the beginning. This form is essentially a musical form, the *rondo*; and though it is no longer true to assert that, as a verse-form, its origin was Moslem, it can safely be said that, in Spain, it was taken over by the Moslems, for the earliest known are not in Spanish but in Arabic.

These *estribillos* or refrains, short as they are, often seem complete poems in themselves. They are not unlike the earliest of all known poems in a Peninsular dialect, those going back to the middle of the eleventh century but only lately discovered—poems in a very primitive form of Spanish (though written in Hebrew or Arabic characters) and used for tail-pieces by medieval Spanish poets writing, as they often did, in the Hebrew or Arabic languages.[9] They also suggest the 3- or 4-line *coplas* of modern *cante jondo* or *cante flamenco*, or the 7-line *coplas* of *seguedillas*: all complete poems in themselves.

These *estribillos* often seem so much more natural and primitive—so much more poetical, even—that the question arises: How far are they original? Are they really by Gil Vicente or Lope de Vega or Góngora, or are they much older, a survival of something much more primitive? It is useless to parry the question by saying that they are folksongs. If we do that, we shall have to explain what folksongs are, and not only what they are now, but what they were in Spain at the beginning of the sixteenth century. Portugal must be considered too, for Gil Vicente who wrote in both languages was himself Portuguese. His poems, with one exception, were published in his plays, one-third of them entirely in Spanish, and rather less than a third in a mixture of Spanish and Portuguese—a dramatic device which must have been most effective in performance. So far as can be determined, he only claimed one of these poems in the traditional style for his own work. His stage-directions are not always clear when they refer to the songs and dances in his plays; yet it is only from the stage-directions that we can form an idea whether he considered the songs his own, or not. The one poem which he actually acknowledged happens to be not only the one which is most like him, but one of the most beautiful poems—and at the same time one of the simplest—in the whole of Spanish literature. It is a song near the end of a mystery-play for Christmas, the *Auto da Sibilla Cassandra*:

> Muy graciosa es la doncella,
> ¡ Como es bella y hermosa !

> None so far as this fair lady !
> No, nor may be richer, rarer.

That is the refrain, the *estribillo*; and the following stanzas ask three different kinds of people—a sailor, a soldier and a shepherd—whether they have ever seen anything more lovely.

> Digas tú, el marinero,
> que en las naves vivías,
> si la nave a la vela o la estrella
> es tan bella.

> Sailor, sailor, tell me truly,
> You who sail in ships for me,
> Is there a ship or sail that's fairer
> Or a star as fair as she?

> Digas tú, el caballero,
> que las armas vestías,
> si el caballo o las armas o la guerra
> es tan bella.

> Soldier, soldier, tell me truly,
> You who wear your arms for me,
> Is there a horse or helm that's fairer,
> Or a charge as fair as she?

> Digas tú, al pastorcico,
> que el ganadico guardas,
> que el ganado o los valles o la sierra
> es tan bella.
>
> Shepherd, shepherd, tell my truly,
> You who keep my sheep for me,
> Is there a flock or field that's fairer,
> Are high hills as fair as she?[10]

The poem, Gil Vicente says, was 'made and set to music' by the author—meaning, probably, that like Robert Burns and Thomas Moore—or like Bellman in Sweden—he wrote it to a tune which already existed.[11] With the other songs in his plays, his share remains 'in the shadowy region of doubt and conjecture in which the authorship of Lope also lies, for the poems which he, too, inserted in his plays'.[12] Another instance of that shadowy region of part-authorship occurs in the first song in the same play.

> Dicen que me case yo:
> No quiero marido, no.[13]
>
> They tell me I must married be:
> There's no man shall marry me.

That *estribillo* may be older than the rest; but the three stanzas express exactly the state of mind of Cassandra in the play; the girl who, wise as a Sibyl and proud as a Sibyl, believes that she, and she alone, is born to be the Virgin Mary. There is a gradual transition between the three stanzas: the first might be sung by any country-girl; the second, by a particular sort of country-girl; and the third, only by Cassandra herself.

3

Gil Vicente and Lope de Vega had an unexampled feeling for popular, country poetry. Sometimes they imitated it; sometimes they wrote variations on it by taking a traditional *estribillo* and writing new stanzas, or sometimes they merely saved an old, popular *estribillo* from being forgotten. Not only did Gil Vicente and Lope de Vega do this, but Camões and Góngora and many other Peninsular poets as well.[14]

Many of the traditional *villancicos* are found in the sixteenth-century music books, arranged for voices, or for voice and *vihuela*, the Spanish lute. But in some we find the older, psalm-like parallel

forms which had been forgotten by educated people for over two
hundred years, but lived on among country people in songs for
dancing. Most of the parallel songs are not in Castilian Spanish
but in Galician Portuguese, though there are some in Spanish which
were sung for madrigals in the sixteenth century. They seem like
the remains of parallel songs of a much earlier date:

> De los álamos vengo, madre,
> de ver como los menea al aire.

> De los álamos de Sevilla,
> de ver a mi linda amiga.

'Mother', he says, 'I've come from the poplar trees, from seeing
how the wind blew in them. From the poplars of Seville, from
seeing my fair little friend.'

The next, however, is a girl's song, a girl looking for a single
gentleman:

> Salga la luna, el caballero,
> Salga la luna y vámonos luego.

> Caballero aventurero,
> Salga la luna por entero.

'Let the moon come out, pretty gentleman: let the moon come
out and off we go. Oh, gentleman adventurer, let the moon come
out to the full.'

In most of these songs, however, we find the parallel form
combined with a refrain, as it is in some of the psalms.[15] In Castille
the refrain generally came first; in Galicia it often did not. It may
consist of two or three lines of verse, or it may be an exclamation
or nonsense-words employed solely for their value in sound. The
pattern is developed further in the Castilian *cossante* by Diego
Hurtado de Mendoza, a song for dancing round the maypole or
the tree of love. The refrain:

> A aquel árbol que mueve la foxa
> algo se le antoxa.

'That tree which moves the leaf has some desire.'

is followed by parallel stanzas in the traditional, Galician-Portuguese
manner:

> Aquel árbol de bel mirar
> faze de manyera, flores quiere dar;
> algo se le antoxa.

> Aquel árbol del bel veer,
> façe de manyera, quiere florecer:
> algo se le antoxa.[16]

'That tree that looks so fine—acts like a barren thing, would give forth flowers—has some desire.'

We are reminded of Rubén Darío, five hundred years later, singing:

> Dichoso el árbol que es apenas sensitivo.

Some of these poems provide pretty problems in textual criticism. The last stanza of *Aquel árbol* is apparently missing, but it can be restored according to the principles of parallel verse. Instead of ending as it does in all modern editions:

> Ya se demuestra, salidlas mirar,
> vengan las damas las frutas cortar:
> algo se le antoxa.

there should be another stanza which might run:

> Ya se demuestra, salidlas a veer
> vengan las damas las frutas coger:
> algo se le antoxa.[17]

The same problem arises with some of the best lyrics of Gil Vicente, e.g.

> Del rosal vengo, mi madre,
> vengo del rosale.
>
> A riberas d'aquel río,
> viera estar rosal florido:
> vengo del rosale.
>
> A riberas d'aquel vado
> viera estar rosal granado:
> vengo del rosale.[18]

In the original edition of Gil Vicente's plays the poem ends by merely repeating the *estribillo* from the beginning, but it is clear that there must be a stanza missing. Vicente's third stanza runs:

> Viera estar rosal florido,
> cogí rosas con suspiro:
> vengo del rosale.

It follows that the missing stanza may have been:

> Viera estar rosal granado
> cogí rosas con cuidado:
> vengo del rosale.

There is probably a stanza missing, too, in a memorable Castilian poem in the *Cancionero musical* of the Royal Palace at Madrid, dating from just before 1500: 'Three Moorish girls enraptured me':

> Tres morillas me enamoran
> en Jaén:
> Axa y Fátima y Marién.[19]

From early times this poem was felt to be incomplete, and attempts were made to restore it. The later version printed by le Strange[20] is already a reconstruction, indeed a re-writing of the whole poem. An attempt to restore it on parallel principles will give better results, though, perhaps, not altogether successfully. The *estribillo* printed in the *Oxford Book of Spanish Verse* is obviously right, and so is the first stanza; but the second stanza should probably be the third, while the fourth is certainly corrupt. The new reading for the second stanza suggested by Carolina Michaelis de Vascon-cellos[21] is:

> Tres morillas tan lozanas
> iban a coger manzanas
> y hallábanlas apañadas
> en Jaén;
> Axa y Fátima y Marién.

This is parallel with the first stanza; and it is now necessary to find one parallel to the third:

> Y hallánbanlas apañadas,
> y tornaban desmaiadas,
> y las colores apagadas
> en Jaén;
> Axa y Fátima y Marién.

4

Primitive songs of this kind existed not only in Galicia and Portugal, but also in León, Asturias and Castille. Yet it should not be forgotten that parallel songs in the Peninsula originally came from (or took root in) the West, while those with a refrain first are pre-dominantly Castilian and influenced by songs originally sung in Spanish Arabic.

Songs of both kinds were included in the great collections: from the *Cancionero general* of 1511 to the *Romancero general* of 1600; but the chief place to look for them is the theatre, above all the theatre of Lope de Vega. Many poets, from that time to this, have felt the attraction of Spanish popular poetry, but none more deeply than Lope. There was no side of Spanish life, and particularly Spanish country life, which he did not touch: the indignant villagers in *Fuente Ovejuna*, the love of traditional ways in *Peribáñez*, the customs, festivals, pilgrimages, weddings, banquets, dances. Above all he was enchanted by the songs which people sang on those occasions. He used popular poetry in different ways. Sometimes he built a whole play out of it; *Peribáñez* is derived from four lines of a ballad. *El caballero de Olmedo* is the story of the old song:

> Que de noche le mataron
> al caballero;
> la gala de Medina,
> la flor de Olmedo.[22]

'It was late last night they murdered him—the *caballero*—the pride of all Medina—the flower of Olmedo'. That was an old song on something which had really happened; one version of the story says that it had happened to an Englishman. In the play, the *caballero*, riding home from Medina at night, hears a man singing about his own—the hearer's—death. The original tune is known; *diferencias* (variations) were written on it by Antonio de Cabezón, the blind musician who accompanied Philip II to England in 1554.

Lope de Vega was not the only Spanish dramatist to use the *romances* and *cantares* of popular poetry. Cervantes did so, in his plays as well as in the *Exemplary Novels* and *Don Quixote*. Tirso de Molina has a most attractive one about reapers and gleaners; even the Mexican Juan Ruiz de Alarcón, remembered them. Not being born in Spain, he had not the same feeling for Spanish country people as Lope de Vega or Tirso de Molina; but when the occasion arose he could make them sing and dance, and the muleteers in *Las paredes oyen* ('Walls have ears') sing a *seguedilla* which is partly in parallel form.

There remains Góngora. He was the best known writer of his time: the favourite of the musicians, the poets' poet. We should not think of him only as the architect of those magnificent baroque constructions, *Polifemo* and *Soledades*. They are the most impressive side of his genius, certainly; but not the only side. Góngora, Alonso says, like Lope and like Tirso, went to the poetry of country people; that was his way of trying to find out how they really thought and felt, not only in Castille and Andalucia but in Galicia and Portugal as well. Góngora did not, like Lope, actually take Galician and Portuguese songs; but he approached, oftener than the others, the characteristically feminine tone of the old Galician and Portuguese poems which have appropriately and wittily been called 'she-shanties'. He used songs sung by people in the country or composed songs himself in the same style; and whether they were his own or not, he combined them with stanzas of his own, some of which haunt the memory for years after one has read them. Others are satirical, burlesque, or frankly comic, like Quevedo's. Among the first is an untranslatable piece of verbal music:

> Dejadme llorar
> orillas de la mar.
>
> Si viniese ahora,
> ahora que estoy sola;
> ola, que no llega la ola!
> Ola, que no quiere llegar!

That, which is included in the *Romancero general*, is in Castilian *villancico* form, though the subject is that of a Galician parallel 'she-shanty'.

Among the satirical poems are the lines beginning with the refrain:

> Trepan los gitanos
> y bailan ellos:
> otro nudo en la bolsa
> mientras que trepan.

'The gipsies are about—and it's they who are dancing!—Another knot in your purse—while they are about!' The poem is satirical; the 'gipsies' were all the people out to rob you in the capital, when it was moved from Madrid to Valladolid and Cervantes was living there finishing *Don Quixote*.

More attractive than any, however, is this:

> Las flores del romero,
> niña Isabel,
> hoy son flores azules,
> mañana serán miel.[23]

Góngora's poem was written in 1609, and was heard, less than twenty years afterwards, sung by someone in the country near Salamanca as follows:

> La flor de romero,
> niña Isabel,
> hoy es flor azul
> y mañana será miel.[24]

M

Was that the original which Góngora had improved, or was it the singer's recollection of what Góngora had actually written?

There is another well-known poem of Góngora's with a distinctly *culto* flavour:

> No son todos ruiseñores
> los que cantan entre flores;
> sino campanitas de plata
> que tocan al alba,
> sino trompeticos de oro
> que hacen la salva
> a los soles que yo adoro ...

'Not all of them are nightingales—those that sing among the flowers. —Only little silver bells—that ring for the sunrise;—only little trumpets of gold—that sound a call—to the suns that I adore.'

Yet even that may have been written with a country tune in the head. Lope wrote a play with the same title; and as lately as 1927, in a village near Salamanca, a folk-dance (*danza de palos*) was being performed to the words.

> No son todos palomitas
> las que pican en el montón ...

There is also a poem, probably not by Góngora though attributed to him, about the man who came round selling peaches and ringing a bell:

> Pasa el melcochero
> salen las mozas
> a los cascabeles,
> a las melcochas
> mozas golosas
> bailan unas y comen otras,
> y al tabaque se llegan todas.

Tabaque is the basket of peaches round which the greedy little girls all gathered dancing or eating.

5

Poetry, in the Peninsula, is the first and most spontaneous of the arts. It enters into people's souls, so that some of the finest verses end by being separated from the poems in which they first appeared, and become refrains. In Spanish and Portuguese poetry we find the ordinary things of everyday life, and the extraordinary things as well: the peaches, the flowers, the gipsies and the sea, with the extraordinary things too: the toils, the revolts, the great collective adventures and the legends. All these things (and it has been said before) have found agreement between people in general and the great writers, for both have made them into poetry. Castille and Portugal have forged links in poetry between their historical traditions and the poetical traditions. In both countries, the language of people in general often seems charged with poetry before a poet uses it; the mere words can provide a poet, whether learned or unlearned, with great and unsuspected resources. There is little of cold intellectuality about them; they were far from that precision and 'algebraical elegance' which a French critic attributed to words in France. To the inventors of popular poetry in Spain and Portugal, the words which came most naturally seem to us now to have more poetical power than they had later. They were still fresh and dewy, and they meant what they said.

NOTES

[1] Dámaso Alonso, *Antología* (Edad Media) Madrid, 1935; Buenos Aires, 1942, No. 37(i).
[2] *Oxford Book of Spanish Verse*, 2 ed. (1940), No. 25.
[3] Alonso, t.c., No. 37(iii).
[4] C. B. Quirós, *La ruta del arcipreste de Hita*, in *La Lectura* XV, 1915, 145–160; reprinted by Alfonso Reyes, *Libro de buen amor* (Madrid, 1917).
[5] *Oxford Book of Spanish Verse*, No. 284. See R. Menéndez Pidal. *Poesía árabe y europea*. (Buenos Aires, 1941), pp. 105–116.
[6] The tune is given by Francisco Salinas, *De musica libri septem* (Salamanca, 1577), p. 306.
[7] Dar as-sultân, the house of the sultan.
[8] Guy le Strange, *Spanish Ballads*, No. 5, Cambridge, 1920.
[9] J. B. Trend, *The Language and History of Spain* (1953), with accompanying bibliography, to which should be added M. Rodrigues Lapa, *Lições de Literatura Portuguesa: Epoca Medieval* 3 ed. (Coimbra, 1952).
[10] *Oxford Book of Spanish Verse*, No. 60. I venture to quote the whole translation, because A. E. Housman told someone that he liked it. See 1616: *English and Spanish Poetry*, II. Concha Méndez y Manuel Altolaguirre. London, 1934.
[11] There are contemporary musical settings of his poems in the *Cancionero musical del Palacio* at Madrid, and in another *Cancionero musical* in the Biblioteca Colombina at Seville; so it is unnecessary to compose new music for them, in a pseudo-Spanish style, for a modern revival of the play. When the original music is lost, it can easily be supplied from either of the contemporary MSS. The first was printed in 1890 and again in recent times. For a full study of the play and its music, see *Music and Letters*, X, No. 2, April 1929.
[12] Alonso, t.c.
[13] *Oxford Book of Spanish Verse*, No. 59.
[14] Idem., Nos. 267–295. See the study by Margit Frenk Alatorre *Sobre los textos poéticos en Juan Vásquez, Mudarra y Narvaez*, in *Nueva Rev. de Filol. Hispánica*, VI, 1952, 33–56.
[15] F. Brittain, *The Medieval Latin and Romance Lyric*. Cambridge, 1937 and 1951, pp. 43–44. The best account of the early Galician-Portuguese poems is that given by Rodrigues Lapa. (See Note 9.)
[16] *Oxford Book of Spanish Verse*, No. 13. The rhythm is not unlike a limerick. *Manyera* 'barren', or perhaps 'artful'.
[17] C. M. de Vasconcellos, *Cancioneiro da Ajuda*, II, 929 (Halle, 1904).
[18] *Oxford Book of Spanish Verse*, No. 268.
[19] Idem., No. 52.
[20] G. le Strange, No. 128.
[21] I. I. Macdonald, *El caballero de Olmedo* (Cambridge, 1934).
[22] *Oxford Book of Spanish Verse*, No. 115.
[23] P. Henríquez Ureña, *La versificación irregular* . . . 2 ed. (Madrid, 1933), p. 217.
[24] *Revista de Filología Española*. XIV, 1927, 417–418.

EPILOGUE

THESE chapters were not isolated lectures and addresses. They have running through them something like a series of musical notes, treated in different ways though on definite principles. The notes are the words and associations of the Spanish language at various times and places, while the series consists of poets speaking Spanish and upholding the continuity of the poetic tradition.

In the early nineteen-twenties I had time in Spain to 'sit about' and listen to people talking: Juan Ramón Jiménez, Unamuno, Pío Baroja, Ortega Gasset, Enrique de Mesa, Pérez de Ayala, Antonio and Manuel Machado, Moreno Villa, Amado and Dámaso Alonso, Pedro Salinas, Jorge Guillén, Vicente Aleixandre, García Lorca, Rafael Alberti, Luis Cernuda, the Mexican Alfonso Reyes and the Spanish composer Manuel de Falla. Most of them were poets or deeply sensitive to poetry, and many were connected with the Institución Libre de Enseñanza or the Residencia de Estudiantes. They naturally included Alberto Jiménez, the Residencia's admirable President: José Castillejo, the great organizer who did so much to widen the opportunities for study abroad of Spanish scientists and scholars; Menéndez Pidal, remote on an Everest of philology; Américo Castro, the fearless and penetrating linguistic historian; Díez-Canedo, the friendly but discerning critic; and above all Cossío, the biographer of El Greco, whom all later writers on the subject— from Maurice Barrès onwards—have pillaged without acknowledgment. The moving spirit of all these had been Don Francisco Giner who, by the time I reached Madrid in 1919, was no more than a memory, though—like the poem about him by Antonio Machado—known to everyone by heart.

It was these men, belonging to what will one day be known for a great period of Spanish thought and endeavour, who gave me my ideas on Spain. Juan Ramón Jiménez and Pío Baroja are not included, because they have already formed separate studies of my own; Rafael Alberti has found better English hands than mine, while an inquiry which I published on Antonio Machado has been carried much farther and with great brilliance by Mrs. Helen Grant. Portuguese, Galicians and Catalans have also been omitted, though they affected poetry in Castilian more than one might think.

172

I have pleasant memories of Eugenio de Castro at Coimbra, Teixeira de Pascoaes at Amarante, and Josep Carner an exile in Mexico. Another Catalan, Eugenio D'Ors, 'Xenius' was an excellent travelling companion in Portugal, and, before that, he had taken me to Majorca and presented me to Joan Alcover, Gabriel Alomar and Sra. de Sureda who had been hostess to Rubén Darío. No one, except Darío's scholarly editor in Mexico, seemed aware of the poem he wrote about her fierce paintings of the contorted, Laocoon-like olive trees:

Los olivos que tu Pilar pintó

which had so frightened him—paintings which she kept in a secret studio across a drawbridge, but one morning showed even to me. They were like the cooled passions of past years: paint flung on the canvas in a rage . . . which is what some might say now of the poems of Rubén Darío. He is certainly out of fashion at the moment, but one of the reasons—perhaps the main reason—is superficial and even frivolous: the dogmatic dislike of many readers of Spanish poetry to six-footed verse. They 'have no happiness in dreaming of Brycelinde'; no memory of Virgil or Ovid, or—in spite of Ezra Pound—of Propertius. It comes of reading Spanish verse as if it were prose—a fashion which dates from the late 'twenties—or of talking of what Spanish poetry is 'about' before the poet's verses are running in one's head. The Spanish-speaking countries of the American continent, however, have brought into their poetry not only six-footed verse but free verse like Vicente Aleixandre in Spain; and with the new rhythm and intonations of their own language come the new ideas of their poetic thought. Rubén Darío belongs equally to Europe and to America; but Alonso Reyes, 'good European' as he is, points to a new, transatlantic sensibility, a new way of thinking and speaking, more clearly exhibited by Ricardo Molinari in Buenos Aires and—in the Portuguese of Brasil—by Manuel Bandeira and Cecilia Meireles.

I have attempted also, by ways like those taken to reach my contemporaries, to approach some of the older poets; but here I should like to emphasize the rarity in Spanish poetry of reliable critical texts—texts which would be accepted and respected by a classical scholar for Latin and Greek. With Luis de León, for instance, or St. Juan de la Cruz, we often do not know what words the poet wrote or how he wrote them; and it may even be suspected that some editors do not know what a 'critical' text implies. Unamuno thought so, at any rate, and thirty years ago he castigated an English editor for his failings in that respect: ¡ *A eso se llama hacer ediciones críticas* ! The later poets need textual criticism no less than the earlier. The Mexican editor of Rubén Darío showed how it might be done; but then, he was a classical scholar. Instead of attending to their texts, writers on Spanish things are apt to fall into various forms of extremism. I have tried to avoid extremist views of all kinds, right as well as left, for that was one of the lessons of the Master: Don Francisco Giner. 'They think', a Spanish schoolmaster remarked not long ago, 'that poetry doesn't matter; but it does. Poetry can change the sensibility of a nation, and therefore its political thought': *Creen ellos que no importa la poesía, pero no es verdad. La poesía puede cambiar la sensibilidad de una nación y por eso su política.*

INDEX